Dedication

To Mom
Mary Louise Lee Gross
Happy 90th Birthday!
*Her children rise up and call her blessed; her husband also, and
he praises her.
Proverbs 31:28*

To Dad
Wylie Watson Gross, Jr.
You've provided for us and been our pillar of strength.
*As for me and my house we will serve the Lord.
Joshua 24.15*

In memory of:
Our dear brother, Chuck
You are never very far from us.

Table of Contents

Foreword

How in this world can an extended family still get together for Sunday lunch? We get asked this question frequently. Through the years people have observed our family and say we have something special. We agree. We've seen a lot of happy times over the years, but we've also experienced much sorrow. We have celebrated weddings, babies, graduations, holidays, and just about any other occasion that strikes our fancy. But we've also experienced illness, deaths, divorce, and lots of disappointments. The ties that bind us all together are our abiding faith, our intentional family times, and our complete dedication to having fun. In our book you will learn about Sunday lunch, a family tradition for five generations and you'll get a flavor of the fun we have. Let me share a bit about the faith that holds us together.

Our parents have always modeled a faith-filled life. Our parents led each of us children to know and love the Lord at an early age. They made learning about people in the Bible interesting, and they taught us that God's word is holy and filled with wisdom and could help us in our daily living. They taught us Bible verses and taught us to claim the truth of them. All of the children and grandchildren know the significance of Philippians 4:13, *I can do all things through Christ who strengthens me.* Our parents told us God has a plan for us and that scripture proves it in Jeremiah 29:11. "For I know the plans I have for you," declares the LORD, "plans to prosper you and not to harm you, plans to give you hope and a future."

Our parents took us children to church from the time we were two weeks old. We attended Sunday school, worship, Training Union, Sunday night service, and Wednesday night prayer meeting. Yes, we were church people. Church going wasn't just for show; our parents have always lived out their faith during the week too. Their lives demonstrate Galatians 5:6 (NIV), *The only thing that counts is faith expressing itself through love.* This love was shown in the home and to others. They instilled in us the way to express our love is through giving, serving, and praying.

3

From the time we received our fifty cent allowance as children, we were taught to tithe. Our parents were always talking about someone in need and the things they could do to help. And then they followed through. We grew up knowing about missions and how important it is to minister to others through our giving and serving. Through Mom's involvement with Women's Missionary Union, we knew all about the mission offerings each year: the Annie Armstrong Easter Offering, the Lottie Moon Christmas Offering, the state and local missions offerings. We heard about missions, we read about missions and we did missions. As a junior high student, every Monday night someone would pick me up and take me to The Children's Home to play the piano. When I was older, I volunteered as a Candy Striper and Red Cross Volunteer in hospitals and nursing homes. Chuck, Lori, and I were taught to use our gifts and talents in service for God. On one occasion the three of us were in charge of the musical devotion for a Sunday school department assembly. I think it was the first and last time that happened! Chuck had learned to the play the guitar and Lori and I played the piano and sang. We muddled through a horrendous version of "Amazing Grace" until Chuck finally decided that we had suffered enough and strummed one last chord that we all instinctively knew was the ending. We didn't say a word; we just went and sat down like it never even happened. "Amazing Grace" is our family song to this day. After our brother Chuck went home to be with Jesus, a family friend made each of us a beautiful framed cross stitched cloth of "Amazing Grace" that hangs in each of our homes.

In addition to giving and serving, our parents taught us the importance of praying. Our prayer models are our parents. Some of my first memories are of my parents on bended knees every night before they went to sleep. My mother is a true prayer angel we affectionately call St. Mary. Mom lives in a constant attitude of prayer. She starts each day with prayer using devotional books that are marked with prayer requests and notes of answered prayer. She prays for each family member by name and with specificity every day. What a beautiful comfort to know that every day of our lives we have been lifted up to God.

Mom is a prayer angel, and Dad is a prayer warrior. He perhaps is the best public prayer I've ever heard. I remember Dad always had a prayer list on his mirror. Each day as he shaved, he prayed for the people on his list. He kept the names of men on his list who were unsaved and prayed faithfully for them. Not too long ago, one of the men who had been on Dad's "list" for over 40 years gave his life to the Lord.

My parents taught us to pray from the time we could speak. "Now I lay me down to sleep. I pray the Lord my soul to keep. If I should die before I wake, I pray the Lord my soul to take." Before every meal, whether at home or away, we said the blessing. We first learned, "God is great. God is good. Let us thank him for our food." We also had the Bread of Life devotional cards in a bread shaped container on our table and we would read a scripture and then a prayer that was printed on the back.

Today with children and grandchildren of our own, we are doing our best to pass on our family faith traditions. Faith is the foundation of our family, and we give thanks to our Heavenly Father for a Christian heritage. We are not a perfect family, and each of us has flaws. But we know that through our failures and our faults, we are loved by a good God and by a family that accepts us for who we are. We are family.

When Mary Louise Lee married Wylie Watson Gross, Jr, our family began. The tradition of Sunday Lunch from the Lee family was carried into the Gross family. Sunday Lunch with its storytelling, fellowship, and the food, is the highlight of our week. It is the tradition that defines us. It is the glue of our family.

We hope you enjoy Lori's beautifully written narrative of our family. It's filled with yarns and tall tales laced with humor and flair that only Sister can give! We also hope you will sample our menus and recipes and will perhaps begin some family traditions of your own!

Aunt Sister (AKA Cathy AKA Cappy)

Acknowledgements

First and foremost we would like to thank Mom and Dad for giving us the material that we had to work with for this book. They have given us a lifetime of treasures, traditions, and training to be good role models to our children and to carry on their legacy of love. They have given us far more than we could ever thank them for, so we do our best to live up to the standards they have set for us and instill in our children the same principles. Thank you, Mom and Dad, for personifying Family.

To Mark and Larry, our husbands, we say thank you for being patient through all the days and nights of sitting in front of our computers while we worked on recipes and recounted tall tales. Mark, you were so good to indulge me when I would laugh out loud from what appeared to be nowhere when I was, in fact, in my memories having a big time with what would pop into my thoughts. Larry, you went above and beyond being the most agreeable person in the world critiquing our menus/recipes; they are all your favorites!

A special thank you is also in order for our family members who have eaten all of our recipes and have weighed in on this project in various and sundry ways. Some of the ways you've helped, you haven't even known you were doing it. Remember all those little cards Aunt Sister has passed out over the years asking for you to write down your favorite meals? Bingo! Found em! Lordhavemercy, you will never know how hard we've laughed reading some of the stuff ya'll wrote down! Priceless! But what's even more priceless, is that you're always there! Sunday after Sunday you continue to want to be a part of our rituals. And these days, you even cook your own recipes. You have no idea how proud of you we are!

To our future family members – we hope our book will give you the history of Sunday Lunch that you need in order for you to understand your heritage and to see that you come from good stock! You come from Southern soul, richly rooted in the legacy of a faith-filled family. You can't buy it; you don't even earn it. It's a gift. Treasure it. Keep the traditions alive!

And to our heavenly Father, Almighty God, thank you. You have so richly blessed us with the gift of being able to put into text a portion of our lives that is too rich to keep to ourselves. For blessing us with not just any family, but, Our Family – we are so grateful. Thank you, Lord, for the sacrifices that were made by our parents long ago to give us everything we ever needed to be able to have the kind of life that we just can't help but want to share.

While we're making acknowledgements, we might as well take this opportunity to recognize each other! We're sisters by birth, but we are the best of friends by choice. Together we have shared life and all the journeys that have led us to where we are. Without each other, we wouldn't have near the fun and we wouldn't have made it through the rough times near as well. So, here's to Sisters –where in tarnation would we be without each other? Don't want to know.

Bon Appetit!
(or as we say in the South, "Enjoy it, ya'll!)

SUNDAY LUNCH

In my family, growing up Southern meant church every Sunday, Wednesday, every revival, tent revival, Sunday Night Singing, Vacation Bible School – Friends, WE WENT TO CHURCH ON VACATION! That's another thing we did Southern Style – Family Vacation. We went to Daytona Beach, Florida every year, stayed at the same motel – The Nomad, and went the 3rd week of June – bank on it. We took side trips, too – camping or Gatlinburg for Labor Day weekend, San Francisco, New York City, Williamsburg, VA, and Canada were also family vacations that have provided lifelong laughter!   But first and foremost we were FAMILY. And as family what we did, we did together – especially eating. Now I am not exaggerating when I say: We have never NOT had Sunday Lunch. It might have been deferred from noon to 6 p.m. but, it was on Sunday and it was called Lunch – Sunday Lunch at night. As our family extended into spouses, and grandchildren, Sunday Lunch stretched into two separate rooms – the dining room for adults and the kitchen for kids. At some point in time, the kids starting filtering back into the dining room because they were curious as to what all the laughing was about. It was their introduction into how our Southern Family had evolved and how much fun we have always had - TOGETHER. You see, it wasn't possible to gather without a tale from the past getting brought up – and then another, and another. Today, we partake of Sunday Lunch in the dining room with adults, grandchildren, and even great-granddaughter, Stella, are all seated around the same table – all seventeen of us, plus babies Will and Wyatt in somebody's lap!

As the grandchildren progressed through their school years, they loved to bring friends to Lunch at Gran's on Sunday, from time to time. To the adults, we considered it a very high form of praise that the kids wanted their friends around and the friends – they liked to come back again and again. In fact, many of the school friends starting addressing us as Aunt, Uncle, Gran and Gaca. We knew we were a special family but having "outsiders" join us and want to come back – it was a sweet confirmation that we were a fun bunch to be around. The age of Social Media put a whole new dynamic to our gatherings because as pictures were posted on media outlets, "friends" would remark about "that gorgeous tablescape", or "my goodness, where did you buy that dessert?" Well, that's the one that'll do you in – Saint Mary doesn't "buy" dessert – it's made from scratch or she doesn't serve it! (Might I add, **that** tradition was understood loud and clear in our growing up days – if you're asked to bring a dessert somewhere, it better have been cooked in your house and put on a serving platter with aluminum foil covering it!) Thus, through word of mouth as well as social media, Sunday Lunch began to be a coveted affair by many. It's not uncommon to be asked throughout the week, "What was lunch on Sunday?" or "What was the tablescape"?

Our family heritage is rich with tradition and so it is our intent to preserve the memories of years together by writing down our menus, recipes, special occasion meals, and in the process, a few tall tales and anecdotes just might find their way to the paper. "Remember the Sabbath to keep it Holy" and then come join us at Gran's for SUNDAY LUNCH.

Cast of Tablemates

Immediate Family Members
Gaca – aka Wonderful Wylie, Daddy, and Jr.
Gran – aka Marvelous Mary, Saint Mary, Mom, Mama, Gransie
Cathy (the first born) – aka Sister, Aunt Sister, Cappy
Larry (Cathy's Husband) – aka L.B.
Chuck (the second born) - aka Chucky and "Our Beloved Chuck" since his passing in 1997
Lori (the third born) – aka – Aunt Lolli
Mark (Lori's Husband) –aka Homer, Uncle Mark

Guest appearances
Joan (Mom & Dad's niece whom they raised from age 5; aka our sister cousin)
Nick (Joan's husband)

Grandchildren	Spouses	Great Grandchildren
Josh	Meredith	Stella, Will
Chase		
Tyler	Amber	Wyatt
Jordan	Kristen	
Kaitlin		
Krista	Adam	

I was raised in a quintessential Southern Baptist-spare-the-rod-spoil-the-child type of upbringing. My mom was a stay at home mom who ran her household as if it were her dream job. Mom grew up with six brothers and sisters and watched three of her brothers go off to war. When her brother, John, went off to war, Mom and Dad took his daughter, Joan, to raise when she was five years old. After the war, Joan wanted to stay with Mom and Dad, so as far as we kids were concerned, Joan was our sister although technically she was our cousin. I didn't get as much time living with Joan because she left for Memphis to go to nursing school when I was a toddler. So, to this day, being around Sister Cousin Joan is always a treat and always fun! Mom's father, a carpenter, worked hard for every penny and even built the house in which she grew up. Her mother, Nanny, raised them all on the foundation of God's Holy Word. According to Mom, Nanny "could pray; Mercy, she could pray." Some of mom's best memories are of her mother and her sitting on the front porch, calling out to God in prayer, praying for the ones who were away at war. Mom said that every morning Nanny would start the day on her knees praying and would wind up standing with her hands raised shoutin' praise to Jesus! When her sister, our Aunt Mildred, was dying, she said, "Mary! I see Momma! She's shoutin!" That moment gave Mom the utmost blessed assurance that she would have a heavenly reunion one day and there would be Joy!

Daddy grew up in a Methodist home where his Mom, our Grandma, was a substitute school teacher and his Dad, our Grandpa, worked at the Post Office for over fifty years until his retirement. Grandpa used to sing in the Post Office Quartet. In Dad's upbringing, education was a priority and from Grandpa, he learned the absolute necessity of working hard at whatever task you were given. I remember as a very young girl going to my Daddy's work and being fascinated just looking around his office. He had an old, yellowed piece of paper taped to his desk that said "If a man should not work, neither shall he eat" (paraphrased from 2 Thessalonians 3:10). When asked, he told me that guidance was instilled in him by his father and after all these years, I not only remember it, I can testify that both Daddy and

11

Grandpa practiced what they preached! Daddy worked hard; then he retired and worked harder. At 88 years old, he needs a day planner to get to all his commitments! Both Mom and Dad had a history with being on the radio. Daddy was the announcer for a weekly radio program called "Let's go to Sunday School" and Mom sang on the radio with the T. Perry Branham Children's Hour from the Tivoli. She still laughs when telling about the time when she was singing in a trio on the radio and she got tickled. And the more she tried to straighten up, the more tickled she got til she finally just quit singing. "Law, I was so embarrassed that I acted up like that – and on LIVE RADIO," she says. All I can say is – if the apple doesn't fall from the tree, between Sister and me, we've left a crop of acting-up all over town!

Let me just give you a little morsel of that apple! Chuck's wife, Teresa, had (and still has) the voice of a song bird! Well, Teresa, Sister and I used to sing in a trio in Church and, on occasion, a funeral or two. Well, when Aunt Mildred died, Mom wanted so much for us girls to sing at her funeral because the whole family had always wanted to hear us sing, etc. (this was a proud momma wanting her girls to sing – pure and simple). However, we were honored to do so and we decided to sing our old faithful go-to song, "Surely the Presence of the Lord is in This Place." The funeral home set-up had the piano perched behind a lattice-work enclosure, hidden from the audience. I don't know why; I'm just telling you it was different and it did not work in our favor that day. So, at our appointed time in the program, we marched ourselves up to the podium, with Aunt Sister our self-appointed chorister, as always. She bobbed her head over towards the invisible pianist, out of habit, I reckon, and the introduction began. The notes that the three of us came out with have yet to be penned on any musical staff in the world! It was horrendous for about two measures till Aunt Sister grumbled, into the microphone, mind you (in which to this day she denies doing it) "oh no. uh –uh" shaking that head. Simultaneously, she is waving that hand over to the invisible pianist trying to stop her from continuing, till she finally leans into that microphone and says "Tammy, we'll start again." So, while the introduction starts up again, I am on my third dying fit with my head straight down

12

looking at the top of the podium, Teresa is stoic but looking, also, at the music; Sister is head up, back straight, getting those chorister hands directing us to come in together and all three of us knowing that if any one of us so much as touched each other we would explode and burst into a fit of laughing hysteria. Start #2 went a little better; however, I, for one was only moving my lips because the note I was supposed to sing was nowhere to be found in my vocal register, my memory, and least of all in my ability to get my act together. At my appointed solo line, I tailed onto Teresa's last line and somehow, by the Grace of Almighty God, I was on key and we pretty much did ok from that point forward. Now I'm telling you the truth that when that day started out it was cold as I don't know what outside and I had on my infernal wool skirt, a sweater with fur – mind you, and of course, I wore those blasted black boots that would heat up an Eskimo and by the time we pranced off that stage I was sweating from head to toe. The three of us filed in that empty pew and all three heads went straight down. We were a combination of mortified, embarrassed and plain old tickled. So, we never even heard the preacher dismiss anybody and only knew it was over when the organ started playing, to which we let out some sounds that come when you're laughing so hard you can't breathe but noise comes out anyway. Well, God love him and bless his heart but one of those ushers thought we were overcome with sadness and moaning, I guess, and he ever so gently brought a box of Kleenex over to us and slipped it under our collective bowed heads and tiptoed off. Friends, that did it! We lost it tee-totally, completely, and to the point that we didn't know whether to stay there or lift our heads up to the public scrutiny that was gonna wait for us outside that funeral home. Well, of course, our precious Mom told us how beautiful it was and how proud she was. Our kids looked at us and said, "What was that?" The preacher said, "I have never laughed in a funeral before but with you three, there's a first time for everything and I just knew that ya'll were wantin' to run!" Mom, we've echoed your Tivoli Radio sentiment! Do you know how many times we have said "Law, I was so embarrassed I acted up like that - and at our Aunt's funeral?" Yep, an apple orchard fell from that tree!

As we began our research for this memoir, Mom (reminder: aka Gran, Saint Mary) began to look through some pictures she had from her and Daddy's (reminder: aka Gaca) early days of marriage. She actually found a picture of her childhood home, taken on a Sunday afternoon when Sunday Lunch was being served. During those days, her family lived mostly in the same neighborhood and walked most places. She had seven brothers and sisters, all of which were married with families. In addition, there were four cars parked in the driveway in that picture leading to the conclusion that "no tellin how many" people were in that house for lunch. She remembers those times to be much the same as what she instilled in our family sixty years ago. There is no better time to gather than for family, food, and fellowship.

What I have given you so far is a little appetizer to what's to follow. Each month will detail a little bit of insight into our family followed by a monthly guide to some of our favorite Sunday lunches. You'll learn a little bit about our tablemates and see what menus we have prepared week to week – we'll call that your entrée. For dessert, we've provided the recipes for our lunch dishes in case you would like to indulge in a little bit of our family's tradition. And for a little tad of something extra-you know how when you're full and about to pop, but you'd like one more little tad of something sweet? Sister and I have created a blog so that we can enlighten you with pictures that relate to some of the tales you're fixin to read. It also gives us an opportunity to document some of the carryin' on that goes on in our family at any given time. Please visit us at sundaylunch.org.

JANUARY

We welcome the New Year on January 1 with family, food, and football. While Sunday Lunch always takes place in the dining room, our Happy New Year meal takes place "downstairs." Downstairs is a completely finished family room complete with a small apartment-style kitchen with a bar for eating –and the only thing stored under that bar are extra casserole dishes and paper plates. This for sure is no bar for libation purposes as Saint Mary would rather go to her heavenly reward than have a drop of liquor in her house. Among other furnishings in this room are a table that seats fourteen, several couches/chairs that face the fireplace and, of course, the TV. We are big on sports in our family and collectively, we represent the Southeastern Conference very well! Among our favorites of the Georgia Bulldogs, the Tennessee Volunteers, and the Auburn Tigers, it is most assured that one of those teams will dictate our eating time according to their game time! The atmosphere is always charged from the anticipation of one of our favorite meals of the year coupled with a heavy dose of football fever. See if you don't agree that this meal is for sure a touchdown with Aunt Sister's Cherry Pie as the winning point after attempt! The only audible you're gonna hear are the various sounds that erupt from a belly full of a good ole southern start to a Happy New Year!

<u>New Year's Day</u>
Mushroom Roast Beef
Mashed Potatoes
Crock Pot Macaroni and Cheese
Black Eyed Peas
Collard Greens
Broccoli Casserole
Oriental Slaw
Corn Muffins
Chow-Chow
Cherry Pie and Ice Cream

Just a side note to this meal – it is the only time that my Mama approves of using paper plates for our family gathering! Seeing that one would have to carry their dishes upstairs to the kitchen dishwasher is completely out of the question after having just spent the day taking down the Christmas tree, putting the decorations in the attic, and then eating ourselves into a comatose state. Yes, those China brand oblong paper plates are totally acceptable on this day; however, plastic utensils remain outlawed.

Even if New Year's Day falls on Saturday, we will still gather for lunch on Sunday. We always say, "Mom, let's just skip this week," or "Let's just have left-overs." The reply is always the same, "Well I'm gonna cook anyway – ya'll just come on, you hear?" So, the first Sunday in January is celebrated just like every other Sunday, in the dining room with our dear family and a renewed focus on the year ahead. I will add that on occasion Aunt Sister will pass around those infernal strips of paper for us to write our New Year's resolution on; she's always gonna keep those strips "til the end of the year" so we can see how we did on our resolutions. Well, I don't believe we've reviewed them a single time! But, I reckon it's a good intention – God love her.

Three different churches are represented among our group and often conversations are generated from church reports. Usually, the first Sunday in January the total has been reported of how much money was collected for the Lottie Moon Christmas offering from the Baptist church goers, and from the Methodist the new sermon series that began on that day is bantered about. When the kids were little, usually a report was given on which new toy was confiscated in Sunday school – it always happened! And it was usually a transformer that Josh had somehow fit into his pocket. Anyway...

By the time, lunch was over, most of us would head home for a long winter's nap having just indulged one more time in the best meal of the week! Those that didn't head home, just stayed there to nap!

January Lunch #1
London Broil
Mashed Potatoes
Corn Casserole
Glazed Carrots
Slaw
Sliced Tomatoes
Sweet Tea
Red Velvet Cake

January Lunch #2
Spanish Spaghetti with Olives
Tossed Salad
Focaccia Bread
Sweet Tea
Chocolate Chip Pound Cake with Ice Cream

Chase, the 2nd grandchild born to Mom and Dad, was born in January. On the day he was born, the temperature had dropped to minus 17 degrees and the city experienced its first winter freeze in many years. Mark and I expected him shortly after Christmas, so the fact that it was January 20 told me all I needed to know about my son – he loved his Mama! His birth date was also the Sunday of Super Bowl XVIIII. He was born just in time for kick off between the Miami Dolphins and the San Francisco 49-ers. Maybe being born on Super Bowl Sunday was a prelude of what was in store for Chase's life. He never wanted anything as much as he did a football, baseball or basketball. He never played with trucks or army men; he only wanted to play ball. He had been watching the Georgia Bulldogs on TV at 5 years old and the next thing I knew, he had gone into his room and gotten out his Sunday clothes, got in his Dad's closet for a red striped tie and put together an outfit just like the coach had worn on the game. He said, "Look, Mom. I'm Vince Dooley." That child would play with starting line ups and play ball outside till he fell over! He would be waiting outside for his daddy to get home from work and have all the equipment ready for whatever sport was in season. They played till dark before they came inside and even then, Chase would try his best to stay out longer. He would say, "Dad, it doesn't matter if it's dark if we can still see the ball." He played basketball, baseball, and football all through his school years and to this day never misses a Georgia Football event! Bless his heart. Chase's birthday meal has been the same since his first birthday. In keeping with that Super Bowl Sunday birth and his subsequent love of all things sports, Chase's birthday meal has always been a game day favorite!

Lori's Homemade Chili with
Oyster Crackers, Fritos, Sour Cream, Shredded Cheese
Hot dogs on the grill with
Mustard, Mayonnaise, relish, ketchup, shredded cheese, diced onions
Sweet Tea
And a theme cake made by Gran

The grandchildren's birthdays are celebrated at their home, hosted by their parents. All the family is invited, of course, and it's always a treat to see the grand unveiling of Gran's birthday cake invention. She has always let each grandchild "design" their own cake. She will ask them to this day, what kind of cake they want and she makes it to specification. As the kids were old enough to drive, they often stopped by Gran and Gaca's house to oversee the icing of the cake or to make suggestions on a design aspect. Nevertheless, the cake is always a surprise to everybody else and we eagerly await what she has come up with to top the year before! Chase's cakes have always been sports related ranging from baseball fields complete with bases and players to a University of Georgia football player. Yes, Gran would replicate a player's jersey, number, and name – right down to the wrist band. She would labor for hours on these cakes and sometimes she even threw it away and started all over if she couldn't get the icing color just right! As he got older, Chase's cakes were always Georgia Bulldog themed, usually a layer cake with an oval G. He has been known to have a birthday pie; however, it, too, is adorned with an oval G. The cake was always brought into the house in a box, carried like it was a porcelain doll and the unveiling always included "How in the world did you do that?" To

18

which she would reply: "Honey, a whole lotta love went into that one!" As if anyone ever doubted that!

Our other January family birthday party was for Chuck. We had the honor of celebrating Chuck's birthday up until age 41. Six months later an accident claimed his life and our family dynamic was forever changed. We know that life will never be the same without him, but we do all we can to honor his life by remembering him, sharing tales about him with his children, and being thankful for the time we did have with him. He left behind his wife, Teresa, his children Tyler and Krista, and a whole lot of memories! His parties were celebrated at Mom and Dad's house, usually downstairs because it was the cold of January and he liked to have the fireplace going. He also liked to set the tone for his party by saying things like "I'd like us to dress up" or "Let's just be real casual." He always provided the element of surprise. Chuck was such a fun person and he loved to make an entrance every chance he got. One year in particular he really took the cake! He arrived just fashionably late and entered the house in his finest tuxedo. I'm here to tell you it was so funny; he just looked at us like it was a normal thing to do and said, "What? I thought we were dressing up." One time, he made his entrance in his pajamas. Obviously that was the year we were gonna be real casual. He was also very traditional about having an actual cake for his birthday. Some of us opted for a pie every now and then on our birthdays instead of a cake and that would just aggravate Chuck to death. He said there was no such thing as a birthday pie and it ought to be mandatory to have a cake. He'd say, "Who ever heard of putting candles on a pie?" Thus, ever the traditionalist, not only did he always want a cake, but it was always a yellow cake with chocolate icing. Kind of boring considering what Mom could do with some flour and a pan, but Lordhavemercy it was good and in true St. Mary style, it was a layer cake and she always iced it in such a way as to put swirls like ocean waves in the icing. It's not possible to see a yellow cake with chocolate icing and not be reminded of our dear Chuck's favorite birthday cake.

January Lunch #3
Chuck's Birthday Meal
Country Style Steak
Mashed Potatoes
Green Bean Casserole
Corn
Slaw
Homemade Rolls
Sweet Tea
Yellow Cake with Chocolate Icing
Ice Cream (anything but vanilla!)

January Lunch #4
Poppy Seed Chicken
Baked Potatoes
Squash Casserole
Apricot Casserole
Congealed Salad
Rolls
Sweet Tea
Strawberry Shortcake Cake

In a family our size, we have a birthday every month, just about. If we don't, we usually find another reason for a "Special" lunch. February's specials are Mark's birthday and, of course, Valentine's Day. Since they are only separated by a couple of days, we combine that celebration and call it "The Love Feast." It works perfectly to have Mark's birthday on this day because his menu never changes from year to year, which works perfectly with the Valentine Theme. Mark's pallet is quite simple and when he finds something he likes – Bingo. No need to mess with it. One thing besides just meat and potatoes that he does really love is Lori's Sweet Potato Casserole. One Sunday, going through the food line, Mark got a pretty good helping of "sweet potatoes." He ate them and oowed and awed the whole time about how good they were. There's so much carryin' on around that table on Sunday that sometimes we tune out the oos and awes. But when the tales quieted down and Mom looked at Mark's plate and saw where those "sweet potatoes" had been, she said, "Well, Marcus, I'm so proud of you that you tried some carrots today!" He wouldn't know carrot soufflé from sweet potatoes in a million years. But he does now.

<u>February Lunch #1</u>
Good Old Fashioned Roast Beef with
Potatoes, Carrots, Onions
Green Peas
Crock Pot Macaroni
Corn Pudding
Slaw
Sour Cream Rolls
Sweet Tea
Peach Cobbler and Ice Cream

<u>February Lunch #2</u>
Mark's Birthday Menu/Love Feast
Cranberry Chicken

21

Mashed Potatoes
Sweet Peas
Corn Casserole
Slaw
Homemade Rolls
Cheesecake with Strawberry topping

So what is the Love Feast? This is Mom and Dad's day to recognize all of us and tell us each how much they love us. It's a good old fashioned Valentine celebration. The tablescape is hearts and roses and little red dishes for holding candy hearts and cinnamon hearts at each place setting. There is a placecard with *Love* written in Gran's handwriting next to your name. When you go to pull out your chair to sit down, there's a gift wrapped in red paper with a white bow. For Cathy and me it's usually a pink or a white top from Talbots. For the kids, a bag of each person's favorite candy, gum, and a personalized treat. And there is always a red plastic heart inside that opens up to reveal a ten dollar bill. The Love Feast is synonymous with Mom and Dad's house. There is more love and generosity in that house than is humanly conceivable. Love is palpable there.

February Lunch #3
Slow Cooker Pork Loin
Mashed Potatoes
Green Peas
Glazed Carrots
Slaw
Sister Shubert Rolls
Sweet Tea
Apple Cobbler and Ice Cream

February Lunch #4
Coca Cola Ham
Twice Baked Potatoes
Broccoli Casserole
Baked Beans
French bread

French Coconut Pie

In recent years, Mom and Dad have made it an annual affair to spend a week in February in Gatlinburg at their timeshare condo. What fun it is for them to have that wood stacked up outside their door and keep a fire lit for a solid week. Cathy and Larry will usually go up on Friday and spend the night with them and Mark and I go early on Saturday and spend that night. Aunt Sister has to get back home to host Sunday Lunch for those that didn't get to go to Gatlinburg! We all gather for breakfast on Saturday morning at the Old Mill or the Pancake Pantry – whatever we choose year to year. It's nice to be away and enjoy the crispness of the winter in the mountains. We girls get in some shopping time and the boys get to cart us around! That's fair, isn't it? Well don't get me wrong – they don't complain; they shop, too! Gatlinburg has a blue million memories for our family because we have been going there for so many years. Our trips date back to the old Mountain View Inn where we would sit in rocking chairs on the porch and dine in the "fancy" Inn dining room. We always took our long dresses to wear to dinner at least one of the nights and the boys had to wear nice clothes, too. Back in those days, going out was such a rarity that to be able to go "fancy" was exciting – not at all anything to dread – boys or girls. We used to go to Gatlinburg for Labor Day weekend with a couple of other families for many years. The last trip I remember was in 1975. Back then, school always started on the Tuesday after Labor Day and so Gatlinburg was our last hoorah. After 1975, some of the kids in our caravan of families had started college and school starting dates changed and Labor Day in Gatlinburg just drifted away. Our family kept going- just not always on Labor Day. When Cathy, Chuck and I got married and had our children, a new Gatlinburg tradition started. We went the week after Christmas for usually a 3 night get away. We either got several adjoining rooms at a hotel or rented a cabin. Not everybody was able to go each year, but the invitation was opened to all who wanted to. Chuck and his family often went on skiing trips during then and even to New York to be a part of Dick Clark's Rockin' New Year's Eve and watch the ball drop a time or two. As the grandchildren got older, they didn't much want to go; they thought Gatlinburg was boring. Knowing we had to make it exciting for them, we did our homework and found a great two story cabin to rent one year that had a huge hot tub and a room where the boys could hook up their Nintendo and play to their heart's content while the rest of us did what we wanted to do. This particular year had the makings of perfection! And for about an hour, it was just that.

The kids were dropped off at the cabin and the adults and Kaitlin and Krista (K & K will from here on out be referred to as "the girls") headed to the outlet mall in two separate cars. Daddy always carted Mom around, "driving Miss Daisy" as it is referred to, and Mark, enjoying shopping as much as anybody drove Cathy, me, and the girls. For some reason, between seven people, we could only come up with two cell phones that had a charged battery – this was a rare, rare occasion as we have always been cell phone ready! However, Mark took Mom's phone and I kept my own. Daddy was in charge of Mom and the girls; he had his phone charging in the car. Now what you need to know about Mark is that he is notorious for getting his words mixed up and calling things by the wrong name. And what you need to know about me is that him doing that drives me absolutely insane! This particular occasion the word snafu was "Eddie Booer" instead of "Eddie Bauer." All he talked about was wanting to go to Eddie Booer and look at pants and shirts. So, he let Cathy and me out in front of that store, went to park the car and was to pick us back up in an hour at the same place. Fast forward 90 minutes. No Mark. And, no answer on his cell phone. Finally, after another 10 or 15 minutes, he answered and don't you know I was fit to be tied and lit into him, like I'm prone to do. I had totally disregarded the obvious strained grunt-like sound in the "Hullo?". I asked him where he was and he said he was at the car trying to get to Eddie Booer. I commented something like (in a higher than necessary pitch):

"Are you kidding me; you still haven't been to Eddie Booer? Where are you?"
Mark: "At the car."
Me: "Where's the car?"

Mark: "Over here. Somewhere just out from where I let ya'll out."
Grunt sound, grunt sound.

Having spotted the car by now, I hung up that phone and proceeded to priss my big self across that parking lot in between cars and people and whatever else got in my way with Aunt Sister not missing a beat right behind me. What we found at the car will be forever ingrained in our memory. Mark was squatted on the ground by the back tire as if he was checking for a flat. One look and I could tell, like how you just know when you really know somebody, that something wasn't right. He looked up at us and said (grunted), "My back went out. This is as far as I got so I've just been pretending I was checking the tires, but I absolutely cannot move and I sure can't get up." Two reactions ensued. Mine – absolutely outdone that his back was messing up our perfect day. Then, Cathy's – immediately springs into action with all the heartfelt compassion that was humanly possible. Then, there's me again-getting out that infernal cell phone.

"Daddy, can you come down here to Eddie Booer and get Mark? Something's wrong with his back and he needs to go back to the cabin".

"Sure, I'll be right there."

Ring. Ring.

"Hey, Hon? I'm looking for an Eddie Booer and I can't find that store."

"I'm sorry, Daddy. It's Eddie Bauer right next to the Disney Store."

"Oh. Ok. I see it. I thought you said Booer or something. Pulling up now."

What happened next was that Daddy became Mark's caretaker. After carefully getting him to the cabin, Daddy helped him in the hot tub. That didn't work. He tried making him comfortable every way he could think of but nothing worked for more than a few minutes. He gave him lots of Aleve. That helped a little. And then he helped him back in the car to come pick us up for dinner. The boys had taken the girls and gone on ahead to make sure we didn't lose our reservation.

We arrived at the restaurant, and Daddy pulled up to let us out of the car. Now, Daddy is the best, most generous, kindest man in the world; however, patience is not his virtue in traffic.

The women folk exited the car while Daddy kept announcing, "Got traffic behind us...need to hurry it up." But there was Mark – stove up, doped up Mark. Just when he got one leg out that car, Daddy thought he had clearance to let off the brake; he clearly did not have clearance. A chorus of STOP! resounded from the rest of us because poor Mark couldn't get that other foot out the car for anything. By this time, Cathy and I have completely lost composure. We had gotten so tickled over my poor husband's misfortune that we walked away to keep him from seeing us. And there is Saint Mary – helping him out that car, walking him up that sidewalk, being so tender and gentle and I was so ashamed of myself for how little I have attended to him, but I can't stop laughing to save my life. We walked into that restaurant and around the corner to where the kids were sitting, saving our table for us and all at the same time those kids put their heads down and acted like they didn't even know us. Here came Cathy and I doubled over laughing, being followed by Gran, holding on to Mark walking the absolute best he could but looking like a stooped over orangutan. He was such a trooper. He felt ok in the chair; he just couldn't stand or walk. Of course, the kids high tailed it out of there when they finished eating and Cathy and I stayed behind to "wait on our change" because we absolutely could not keep it together in front of him. While Daddy retrieved the car, Saint Mary walked the patient out – not before she admonished Aunt Sister and me that we should be ashamed of ourselves. And we were. It just didn't look like it. There is always icing on the cake (if it's any good) and it came just as we exited the restaurant many steps behind the patient and his caretaker mother-in-law. Two ladies sitting on a bench said "Ooh. He don't look good." To which the other replied. "Um, somebody had too much to drink." Icing on the cake!

(By the way, a visit to the Extended Care, two shots of muscle relaxer/pain killers, 3 days asleep in the bed – he was good as new.)

MARCH

March brings such a welcomed relief from winter to our warm weather oriented family and it's always nice to bring out the spring décor. Cathy's birthday is in March and we love to put on a tablescape that's pink, pink, and pink and sprinkled with pearls and, of course, a tiara for the Queen. For milestone birthdays (which I can assure you they have all become milestones the older we get) Saint Mary pulls out all the stops. She has saved every report card, Easter dress, childhood I Love You note, and memorabilia that any of us ever had as a child. At the 40th birthday milestone, for each of us, Mom decorated the living room with all manner of childhood memorabilia and even had a clothes rack in which she displayed various Sunday suits and shoes of Chuck's, Sunday and Easter dresses that Cathy and I wore, Prom Dresses, and piano recital regalia. To top it off, she put together a photo album, and by photo album I mean a Webster sized dictionary photo album that celebrated our life in pictures from birth to 40. It was spectacular and a coveted memory that we, along with our children, love to look at from time to time. Another thing our precious Mama does is write each of us a *Birthday Letter* and by everybody I mean all of us including grandchildren and great-grandchildren. Mama writes it; daddy types it. Together, they make a collage of pictures that she has taken over the past year that serves as a little picture diary of the honoree's life since the last birthday and it is included with the letter. It is a precious, priceless account of a mother's love for her children.

Besides Sister's birthday, the spring reminds me of some of our favorite vacations. Spring break usually came in March and we headed to Destin where we took up residence at the Army Recreation Center that was only available to active or retired military. Since Daddy is a retired Lt. Colonel in the Air National Guard, each year we were able to rent a cabin we affectionately named "the barracks." We would usually arrive in shifts as Mom and Dad would leave on Saturday and take Josh and Jordan (Cathy's boys) and the rest of us would follow on Tuesday or Wednesday of the next week. One particular year, the biggest snow storm of the century was forecast to hit the day Vehicle1 was scheduled to leave. So, in true "get ahead of the game" Lt. Colonel Mentality, Gran, Gaca, and the boys headed for Destin to outrun the snow storm. They made it – barely. Montgomery had gotten hit an hour or so before they got that far and as the Colonel's Cadillac passed through, he took some souvenirs in the form a fence post and a lot of dug up yards where the road stopped being real visible. It was an adventure for that crew, to say the least; however, back at home it was an adventure of epic proportions. That snowstorm left us with a foot of snow, downed power lines, and a huge motivation to get to the beach. So Vehicles 2 & 3 left out on Tuesday headed for the sunshine. That was the coldest spring break I can remember. But I'm telling you the truth that where there's a will there is a way and if we want to sit in the sun and get a little color on us, then you better believe its gonna happen. So, Mark, Sister, and I got out our blankets, spread 'em on the ground and propped ourselves up against the side of the barracks for a wind shield and there we lay to get us a tan. When the wind would whip really hard, we rolled up in those blankets till it passed and then went right back to sitting straight up, legs out, books opened.

We did all kinds of things at the Barracks that we didn't usually do, except for one thing – Daddy always lost his glasses in the water. He lost them in the ocean, the bay, the lake...it just happened despite all of us hollerin' "Wait! Take your glasses off!" He'd inevitably come up out of the watering sayin', "Well, dern" and the rest was us would be shaking our heads and rolling our eyes. However, in Destin we did something we would never do at home - we rented a pontoon boat. Now, I'm telling you this – the boat ride was fun; anchoring out in the Bay- that was also fun. The process of getting in and out of the boat slip was harrowing at best. A time or two, this is the point in which Daddy would lose his sunglasses, bending over trying to keep the side of the boat from hitting the dock. Might I add that not only did that boat hit the dock; we usually left a part of that dock down the side of those pontoons. The kids didn't have a clue; the adults sat in the back predicting the outcome and getting it right – every time. Sometimes it was too cold to go out in the Pontoon but the weather did not matter to the kids; they played ball, played on the playground, swam, and Jordan met his first girlfriend. She was a little French girl named, Marie, and she called him Jor-Dan, which has stuck with him to this day. They shared frozen Snicker bars as a treat on their last day together. Years later when Cathy was packing up Jordan's room when they were moving, she found that empty Snickers box among his treasures. God love him. Chuck and Teresa didn't stay in the barracks- they opted for the adjoining hotel part of the Recreation Center. So, being an early riser and having no kitchen, Chuck would often slip off to The Donut Hole and bring back a bag of apple fritters for breakfast and he was known to pick up a key lime pie while he was there for an after dinner treat. He even set out one day for the Sexton's Seafood and brought back fresh fish to cook...just in case anybody wanted it. He was the ultimate foodie. Side note – to this day, we have key lime pie on our beach trips. It's just one of those things that makes us smile on the inside. Just before we left the barracks each year, we would gather for a family photo on the rocks in front of the bay and it never failed that the wind kicked up about shutter time and the best we got sometimes was hands in the air holding our hair down – but we were still smiling! We headed home in a caravan wondering which car would get a speeding ticket by the Alabama State Patrol; it was usually mine.

Favorite Destin Restaurants: The Back Porch, The Donut Hole, Silver Beach Inn (for breakfast), Harry T's, Fuddpuckers, and the Gelato stand at the outlet mall.

<u>March Lunch #1</u>
Milanese Chicken
Crash Potatoes
Green Beans
Squash Casserole
Salad
Rolls
Sweet Tea
Cream Cheese Key Lime Pie
Homemade whipped cream

March Lunch #2
Chicken with chipped beef
Garlic Mashed Potatoes
Broiled Asparagus
Mixed Vegetable Casserole
Salad with fixings
Sour Dough Bread
Sweet Tea
Bread Pudding

March Lunch #3
Sliced Roast Beef
Texas Potatoes
Broccoli Casserole
White shoepeg corn
Sour Cream Rolls
Sweet Tea
Chart House Mudd Pie

March Lunch #4 - **Cathy's Birthday**
Grilled Chicken
Rice Casserole
Green Beans
Glazed Carrots
Tossed Salad
Rolls
Sweet Tea
Strawberry Cake with Ice Cream

March Lunch #5
Swiss Steak
Mashed Potatoes
Green Beans
Squash Casserole
Slaw
Rolls
Sweet Tea
Grandma's Oatmeal Cake

EASTER

Easter Sunday, like most aspects of our family's heritage, is steeped in tradition. Our menu has stood the test of time and the only thing that has changed is the presence of "the bunny cake." While the grandchildren were young, their Gran always made a coconut cake and a bunny cake for them. It was a white cake with white icing in the shape of an Easter bunny complete with coconut flakes for the fur, jelly beans for the eyes, twizzlers for the whiskers, and pink food coloring for the ears and nose. As the kids got older, the bunny cake disappeared in favor of Cheesecake. As soon as we arrived at Gran's for lunch, each family diligently took their place in front of the oak tree that served as the back drop for family pictures through the years. We have Easter pictures from when the children were born right up to them holding their own children. An Easter egg hunt always ensued after lunch and Gran and Gaca always made sure to hide the eggs on Saturday when it became apparent some of the grandkids had roving eyes during hiding time! The hunted eggs had coin money in them with "the golden egg" having what the kids called "real money." Whether it was $1 or $10, the thrill of finding that one golden egg was worth more than what money was in it. One year, Jordan found the prize but it had nothing to do with anything Gran or Gaca hid. Just when all the kids had their baskets full and the golden egg was still out there, Jordan came running around the side of the house yelling, "Look!" Assuming he had found the Golden egg, we all ran over to where he was and what he had in his hand was a dead rat he was holding by the tail! We screamed and scattered and as far as I know, that golden egg is still out in that yard somewhere! Hairstyles and Easter fashions have changed over the years; but, one thing that has been as deeply rooted in our family as the roots in that old oak tree is our celebration of Easter as the Resurrection of our Lord Jesus Christ. He is Risen; He is Risen indeed.

Easter Meal

Coca-Cola Pulled Ham
Potato Salad
Baked Beans
Pineapple Casserole
Deviled Eggs
Chips
Cheese Bread
Sweet Tea
Coconut Cake
Cheese Cake

APRIL

Since Easter is sometimes in March and sometimes in April, the tablescape stays in the Bunny theme for both months. Over the years, the bunny collection has grown from simple ceramic bunnies to the now more elaborate Fitz and Floyd Mr. and Mrs. Bunny collection. In recent years, truth be known, I've seen some Jim Shore bunnies sitting around. Jim Shore has typically been responsible for the snow people that adorn our home in the winter months. Daddy started a tradition of giving those to Cathy and me years ago. Saint Mary always enjoys switching up the place cards between the bunny themes, the spring flower theme or just wrapping the napkins in a spring colored ribbon.

April 1 became the best day of the month in 2011 when Josh and Meredith became the parents of Stella Grace Robbs. Stella is the first Great Grandchild to Gran and Gaca, first Grandchild to Cappy, and the first Great Niece to Mark and me. She instantly became the light in our lives and her little feet don't hit the ground when we are all together. To Stella, Gran is Gransie, Cathy is Cappy, and Lori is Aunt Lolli, Mark is Uncle Mark and might I add, there is an attachment at the hip to those two. Stella brings out the best in all of us. She reminds us of how easy it is to love and how the simple things in life are really the best things. She has brought more happiness and joy into our lives than anyone could have ever imagined. To the cousins, Stella is the "be all to end all." Her Uncle Jordan is so smitten with her that you would be hard pressed to know that she wasn't his daughter. I'm sure "Uncle Jordy" has instilled in Stella her attitude of "no fear." The higher he throws her, the higher she wants to go! Aunt Kristen is the one who gets in the floor and paints with her or walks in the yard and picks flowers wherever Stella leads. Krista, the educator, sits with her and looks at books, and Tyler and Amber make mental notes of what it will be like when they have their little one. Chase, aka "Hoss" to Stella, is who sits for long periods of time with her in his lap and they watch videos on his phone. They have their special ones; but, the favorites are music where she has learned to sing along and even mimic the gestures of the artists in the video. Kaitlin is in charge of hair bows and hair-dos. That side pony always gets going when those two are together. As Kaitlin learned from her own childhood – we do not leave home without a hair bow. Therefore, Stella Grace is adorned at all times, even if it has to be a makeshift bow.

<u>April Lunch #1</u>
S & W Baked Spaghetti
Salad
Garlic Bread
Sweet Tea
Fudge Brownies
Ice Cream

<u>April Lunch #2</u>
Apricot Chicken
Long Grain & Wild Rice
Broccoli Casserole
Corn Casserole
Rolls
Sweet Tea
Lena's Chocolate Cake
Ice Cream

One thing that Daddy used to always do in the spring is take Cathy, Teresa and I to lunch at The Walden Club. It was always such a treat to go there for any occasion but lunch with daddy was even more extra special. Now while we were off enjoying our afternoon of pampering, mom was babysitting our boys – all four of them. We worried the first time that it would be too much for her to keep all of them by herself. However, our fears were promptly obliterated when we came home to find that she had them all lined up on the back porch hitting fly balls and grounders to them and then pitching to them so they could hit. They were orderly, fully engaged, and aggravated that we had come back for them! Mom taught all of those boys to play ball. She would spend hours outside with them; I think they gave out before she did.

When the girls were born and thrown into the mix, they spent their time in the kitchen with their Gran making sugar cookies. To this day, the girls still go over the week before Christmas and make sugar cookies, using the same cookie cutters they have had all these years and they use lots of icing and sprinkles! As the boys got older, Mom and Dad would take all of them to a Braves game and spend the night in Atlanta. Of course, Gran would take hundreds (no exaggeration) of pictures to document the weekend and when they got back, she would have the pictures printed and make each of them a photo album commemorating the trip. The first page of the album was always the four of them in front of the car with a poster that said, "Off to See the Braves" and the year. What a treasure to look at those albums from time to time and be reminded of how much Mom and Dad have invested in not only our lives, but the lives of our children. For the girls, they took them on a weekend trip to Pigeon Forge to Dollywood! They even rode the rides with them. The girls got the same kind of commemorative photo album and to this day, they talk about those trips! Whether it was the boys at the Braves game or the girls in Dollywood, all the kids returned home with a souvenir of their choosing and stories to last till the next year. Our children never doubt the stories we tell about our childhood because they have also experienced the devotion, the fun, the sacrifices, just the feeling of absolute assurance that they are loved beyond imagination.

<u>April Lunch #3</u>
Beef Brisket
Mashed Potatoes
Green Beans
Corn on the Cob
Slaw
Texas Toast
Sweet Tea
WMU Pie

(Side note-my Mama used to host the WMU (Women's Missionary Union) meetings at our house and she would always make this "Chocolate Wafer Pie". However, I have always called it WMU pie because that's the only time I ever saw it and don't you know I couldn't have any of it unless there was some left over. According to my Mama, "we never cut into a dish of anything before it's presented to its intended audience." And, yes, there was always a piece left over. I bet it was Mama's.)

<u>April Lunch #4</u>
Grans Homemade Chicken Fingers
Homemade Honey Mustard Dipping Sauce
Mashed Potatoes
Baked Beans
Lays Plain Potato Chips
Salad with Fixings
Rolls
Sweet Tea
Chocolate Swirl Cheesecake

MAY

The first week in May has been dubbed "Ocean's East Week" for over 25 years. Ocean East is the name of the Condominium Resort where Mom and Dad bought a timeshare unit many years ago and the first week of May is their time to be there. Because of that, the family has gone together many of those years and, yes, we all stay in the same condo. As the boys got older, they were allowed their own room; however, after about two trips with that arrangement, they lost those privileges. From Pringle cans halting the elevators to prank calls all over the resort we thought it best to keep close quarters again. Some years, we took a day and drove to Disney World and if we didn't go to the park, we at least ate at The Hard Rock Café. The one staple on our Ocean East trip was that Gran would take the kids to Pirate's Cove to play miniature golf. For some reason, at Pirate's Cove, the wind blew harder there than anywhere else in the city – I'd swear to it. However, bundled up in jackets, Gran and Gaca headed out to play golf with all the kids. Most of the time Gran won, which would just wear the boys out. The girls were more interested in NOT getting a hole in one so that they keep their golf ball! One year, the boys were old enough to rent 4-wheelers for the beach. Don't you know they thought they were big stuff? Gran and Gaca even rode on them! We had our favorite restaurants that we went to where we always ate way too much and said we wouldn't do that again – but we did. Mark, who doesn't eat salad (or anything else green), always predicted the first comments that would be made after the salad was served: "Oh, goodness, I'm already full; I wish I'd just ordered salad." He got it right every time! Some of our favorite places were Marko's, where they served a little tiny cone of orange sherbet before the main course to "cleanse the pallet." We loved to go to Park's where they served complimentary Seafood Dip and Fish chowder and the kids got paper placemats that had the map of Florida on them, in which they drew various additions on the map! We enjoyed Julian's for many years where we dressed to the 9's for our "fancy" night out. They had a Polynesian décor and live entertainment in the form of a singer who played the organ and sang tunes like "Welcome to My World"; I can hear it right now. We had to be strategic about where we sat in Julian's because along with their Polynesian décor, they had Totem poles placed around the restaurant and Chase was horrified of them. He turned around one time and caught site of one and came completely apart right there in front of God and everybody, and I tried everything I knew to calm him down before that complimentary relish tray finally got to our table and he was occupied with carrot sticks and dip. We still enjoy eating at Aunt Catfish, where "Cousin" so and so will be your waitress and the "fixins bar" is still served with cheese grits, baked apples, baked beans, slaw, and cornbread. That's another one of those times when various rumbles can be heard regarding wishing they'd ordered just the salad and fixins and no entrée.

In our growing up years, our Uncle Jim and Aunt Virginia lived in Daytona and taught us how to enjoy the Dog Races. Aunt Virginia could pick a winner every time! Now, you need to know that Saint Mary and Daddy never did do the dog races; as Southern Baptists, they don't gamble. However, as delinquent children, Cathy, Chuck and I went – just to spend time with our Aunt and Uncle. Umhummmmm. And if we came home with a little money...well, I think it was just ice cream money from the relatives. Let's say it was. Now one year we were in Daytona when Hurricane David came through. It was like mayhem. All the windows were getting boarded up, the pool furniture put in the pool to keep it from flying around, and cars lining up to get out of there. Well, being as Uncle Jim and Aunt Virginia were there, we weren't going to leave town until we went and checked on them. It took forever to get over to where they lived because traffic was at a standstill everywhere, don't you know. When we finally got there, we found them to be in great hands.....in Chattanooga with the rest of the family. They heard about Hurricane David and high tailed it out of there two days earlier! That's the difference between locals and tourists – this was by no means their first rodeo or dog show – whatever.

May is a popular month in our family for celebrations. Cathy's husband, Larry, has a birthday in May and he and Cathy also got married in May. Mark and I got married in May as well.

Our wedding was thirty-two years ago, while Cathy and Larry's wedding was more recent. What a blessed event when those two tied the knot! It was an intimate affair with just family and a few close friends, but we were all there thinking the same thing-"It's about time!" We have loved Larry being in our family for several years and we have very much wanted him to be our official Brother-in-law, Uncle, Son-in-law, and Papa Larry. Now here's what I can tell you about Larry (aka LB). He observes. In all the carryin' on that goes on when we are all together, he just takes it all in. When he has something to say, he says it. If he doesn't, he is content to just sit and be a part of it all. Mostly, he can be found in the kitchen after dinner loading the dishwasher, along with Mark. And I can also tell you this about my brother-in-law. He would do anything in the world for anybody at any time. Good as gold, he is. Just a little tidbit to add about their wedding ceremony – Aunt Sister requested that the family do "The Cupid Shuffle" at the reception. So, for a couple of months leading up to the wedding, those in attendance at Sunday Lunch would commence to practicing the dance after we ate. Those who weren't in attendance were expected to practice sometime during the week. Why were they expected to do that? Because the dance request came from Aunt Sister and we do not let Aunt Sister down. We go all in. So, at the appointed time at the reception, the DJ started the music and our whole family, complete with Daddy's holding infants, danced The Cupid Shuffle. Even St. Mary cut that rug. So what we had was a family dance party – with ages from nine months to ninety years. It was so much fun! It was very much indicative of our family – some kicks, some turns, a little bit of shuffling, a whole lot of laughing, all in rhythm.

<u>May Lunch #1</u>
Larry Birthday Dinner
Country Style Steak
Mashed Potatoes
Green Beans
Macaroni and Cheese
Beets

Slaw
Sweet Tea
Strawberry Cake and Ice Cream

May is also the month in which Tyler Watson Gross was born to Chuck and Teresa. He is the third grandchild born to Gran and Gaca. Christmas of 1984 was celebrated with one Grandchild, Josh. Christmas of 1985 was celebrated with four Grandsons. Chase (January), Tyler (May), and Jordan (September) were all born four months apart that year. So, we like to joke that for Christmas 1985, Cathy, Chuck and I gave Mom and Dad grandsons. Tyler was always the conscientious one of the grandsons. While the others played with toys or balls, Tyler played with tools. He loved the Playschool learning tools which was a form of imitation of his dad. As he grew older, he liked to go on job sites with his dad and ultimately followed in his footsteps both by going away to Auburn for college and by becoming an engineer. One year at "Career Day" in elementary school, Tyler invited his Dad to come and speak to his class. Other parents that came to speak included a doctor, a lawyer, and a fireman. Chuck owned a heating & air business. When the teacher asked Tyler to introduce his dad as the speaker, she said, "Tyler, what does your Daddy do?" To which Tyler replied, "Nothing. He's just a worker man." Needless to say, that one has carried us for years! Tyler married God's perfect match for him, Amber. Amber is a beautiful Christian woman who blesses our family with her beauty and her gentle spirit. We are so thankful for the wife she is to Tyler and for the way she embraces our family. This year, they became parents to precious Wyatt.

Gran was quite industrial with a few cake creations for Tyler during his growing up years. One in particular that was outstanding was a Lawn Mower cake. She even "engineered" a handle that came up out of the cake. The icing was green and textured to look like grass; the body of the mower was yellow. It felt like a sin to cut it and eat it! But being that the birthday boy was two and being that we are who we are, it was eaten – grass and all. Tyler's birthdays were the biggest collection of different cakes; he had a dinosaur cake one year with Tylersaurus written across the front, a wrestling ring one year, and even an ice hockey cake when he was ten. As he got older, his cakes were themed for the Auburn Tigers and usually a cheesecake.

May Lunch #2
Tyler's Birthday Meal
Grilled Chicken (Honey Mustard)
Baked Potatoes with all the fixings
(Butter, sour cream, bacon pieces)
Broccoli Casserole
Corn Casserole
Asian Slaw
Rolls
Sweet Tea
Cheesecake

May Lunch #3
Chicken Cordon Blue
Jasmine Rice
Steamed Broccoli
Glazed carrots
Salad
Rolls
Sweet Tea
Oatmeal Pie

May Lunch #4
Chicken Pot Pie
Baked Potatoes
Roasted Vegetables
Salad
Homemade Italian Bread
Sweet Tea
Apple Pie with Ice Cream

JUNE

Our family loves the summer! We do outside activities as much as possible and love our time at the beach or the pool or just having our meal on the back porch. Back in the day, Daddy got the opportunity to travel to some big conventions when he served on the local school board. For three years, Mom and Dad took one of us each year to the Convention; Cathy went with them to Los Angeles, Chuck went with them to Houston, and I got to go to Miami. One year, the Convention was going to be held in San Francisco and the whole family got to go! And I'm telling you the truth that when we three siblings got together, funny found us. We had flown to San Francisco and rented a car at the airport. It was very late on a Saturday night when we got there. With the time change and doing a little sightseeing we went to bed later than usual. When we woke up the next morning, Mom and Dad were gone! My first thought was that they went to get breakfast. The reality was that it was Sunday and God love their hearts, they had gone to church – as the note on the door said. What I thought was – "But, I'm hungry." What Chuck thought was "They left the car keys; let's go do something." Looking to Cathy for approval, she already had her shoulder strap purse on. Five minutes later, the three of us were in a rental car with Chuck driving and we were winding around San Francisco taking it all in! Cathy and Chuck were in the front (of course) and they were talking map jargon and I was all eyeballs in the backseat. At some point Chuck turned around and told me to "get ready-here comes the bridge." I looked up and what we were approaching was the Golden Gate Bridge! I will never forget how massive it looked as we approached it but, being on it and looking up at those cables was breathtaking! We all three screamed! We could not believe we were on the Golden Gate Bridge! It is such a memory that we got to share all together. Every time I see that bridge on TV or in movies, I think about Chuck driving us over that bridge and Cathy saying over and over "I can't believe it; I just can't believe it!" I have no idea how long we were gone but it must have been a while because when we got back to the hotel, Mom and Dad had been out of church too long and whatever peace was afforded them in that church, we had counter acted it because we never thought to leave them a note on the door when we left for our adventure. All they knew was that when they got back, there were no kids and no rental car. And remember – no cell phones back then!! Lucky for us, they were so happy to see us upon our arrival that any aggravation they had dissipated. They just knew, as parents do, that our adventure over that bridge didn't need cold water thrown on it and with a gentle nudge, we didn't go off anymore without leaving a note.

At some point in time, we changed our hotel and stayed in a Ramada Inn on Fisherman's Wharf for the remainder of our trip. We made lots of memories! Cathy had long hair that reached below her waist and she was a dead ringer for Karen Valentine, star of the TV show *Room 222*, which was very popular during that time. We were waiting outside the hotel for Daddy to bring the car up from the garage so we could go to dinner when all Cathy and Chuck needed to hear was a passerby say, "That girl looks like Karen Valentine." They connived and Chuck sent Cathy back into the hotel lobby and stood out on the curb like he was looking for somebody. He turned around and motioned for her to come out and started talking to her (too loud) calling her "Karen." It worked like a charm. You could hear people chatting and realizing they were looking at a movie star and started asking her for her autograph. AND SHE GAVE IT TO THEM! When Chuck saw Daddy pulling around the building to pick us up, he told the by-standers, "No more autographs, please," opened the back door of our car, and ushered her in it! We climbed in that car and drove off, trying to tell Daddy what had happened, as Mom and I had observed the whole thing in the distance and between the laughing and the talking all at one time, we got it out. It wasn't the last time in San Francisco that she signed an autograph! Chuck was a little popular that trip, too. He was being irritable one afternoon and wouldn't walk with the rest of us along the wharf. All of a sudden a gentleman noticed him walking alone and propositioned him. You have never seen anybody walk-run-scoot as fast as he did to catch up with his family. He did everything but hold our hand and I promise you he never walked solo again till we got back home! On the morning we were checking out of the Ramada, our room smelled horrible. I mean it was wretched! Nobody could figure out what it was; but we were glad to be getting out of it. As Daddy did his usual last check around the room, under beds, behind doors, etc., he opened the desk drawer to find a HUGE lobster in the drawer. Chuck had bought it down on the wharf just so he could say he did and then didn't know what to do with it so he put it in the drawer. Now this may have happened on the day he got caught walking alone and that would explain his irrational behavior; otherwise, he was just being Chuck and thought it would be a waste to throw that lobster away! All these years later, it's still a funny memory and I can still remember that smell! We've often wondered what the housekeeper must have thought!

June Lunch #1
Crock Pot Beef Bourguignon
Garlic Mashed potatoes
Green Beans
Yellow Corn
Beets
Slaw
Rolls
Sweet Tea
Best Ever Chocolate Pie

Josh was born in June and being he was the first grandchild to be born it was going to be a HUGE event even if he hadn't been born in the midst of a wedding going on. Friends, everything that happens to us seems to come about in a fanfare when you'd think a simple occasion would do. Cathy's brother-in-law was getting married on this particular day and she was singing in the wedding. Bill, Josh's dad was, of course, a groomsman for his brother. Just about prelude time, Cathy stands up with lots of water running down her leg. Now, you need to know that Princess Cathy would never allow herself a bladder too full to spill, so what we had going on here was a water break. Being that the little church house where we were had no phone and the nearest neighbor was "over yonder," somebody had to set out "over yonder" to use a house phone to call the Dr. Guess who that was? SISTER!! Yes, the mother-to-be! The Dr. said she could stay through the wedding if she wasn't having contractions, but get to the hospital as soon as it was over. So, she sat tight on the front pew while the processional proceeded and at her time to sing, Bill took off his Tuxedo coat, she put it on, and stood there belting out The Lord's Prayer in a blue dress, tuxedo coat, and a wet backside. The Bride and Groom kissed, got presented to the audience and right after they got good and out of that church, Cathy was carried out to a waiting car and carted 30 miles to the hospital. As the rest of us arrived at the hospital throughout the evening, the other families in the waiting room had real confused looks on their faces as all the wedding attire and tuxes made their way into the waiting room. Finally, someone said, "Who was in a wedding?" to which Daddy simply replied, "The mother and father." Confusion looks so funny on some people. Back in 1981 a "mother and father" coming to labor and delivery from the wedding was not so much an accepted occurrence as it might be in today's society. We got a good laugh out of it for years to come.

Growing up, Josh loved Transformers action figures, Madden Football, and can still quote the movie *Top Gun* from start to finish. He also loved it when *Monday Night Raw* came on and the boys would come over to watch. Now that wrestling thing caused a ruckus because the four boys liked to act out what they had seen on TV. Listen here- those boys made Goldberg and Stone Cold Steve Austin look like Cinderella and Snow White. And to top it off, Stone Cold Steve Austin had as his slogan, "Austin 3:16." (Now that's just awful!) One time, Gran had taken the boys to buy them a treat (like she did so often), and they saw a t-shirt with "Austin 3:16" on it. Those boys thought they could con Gran into getting them a "Christian" t-shirt. Didn't happen. She was way smarter than they knew and flat told them she wasn't contributing to that kind of blasphemy. Umhumm –"Train up a child..." Amen. They were totally defeated and they knew it! Josh has always been quite the scholar and as he grew up was found to have a particular interest in all things political. He still laughs easily, is up for a good joke on somebody, and loyal to a T to the Tennessee

Volunteers. Josh found his perfect match in Meredith and together they gave us Stella and Will. Meredith says she married "her best friend" when she married Josh and it shows. She is a beautiful, talented, Christian young woman who always offers to help with anything from Sunday Lunch to decorating – and we always take her up on it!

Josh's birthday cake was typically baseball themed. It was complete with positional players and a batter. If Gran couldn't find player figures in the colors of the team he wanted, she just painted over the ones she could find. It was really hard to cut those cakes and ruin them. They needed to be on exhibit! As he got older, Josh's cake was a Tennessee Vol theme. Josh preferred cheesecake and on top would be a Gran-fashioned Power T.

<u>June Lunch #2</u>
Josh's birthday Meal
Boston Butt – shredded
Potato Salad – Robbs Family Recipe
Baked Beans
Chips (Lays Wavy)
Slaw
Bar B Q sauce
Fresh Cut Watermelon
Yellow Cake with chocolate icing
Homemade Ice Cream

<u>June Lunch #3</u>
Slow Cooker Pork Loin
Hash Brown Casserole
Baked Beans
Pineapple Casserole
Dinner Rolls
Sweet Tea
Lemonade Pie

June Lunch #4
Balsamic Grilled Chicken
Long Grain Wild Rice
Carrot Soufflé
Broiled Asparagus
Grilled Corn
Salad
Sweet Tea
Fudge Pie and ice cream

JULY

Patriotism runs high in our family and it's no wonder because Mom's brothers were veterans and Daddy was in the Air National Guard until he retired as a Lt. Colonel. We knew the sacrifices made by the veterans and we understood clearly the privilege we have of living in the United States of America. Our children have inherited from each of us the pride and privilege of being a part of the Red, White, and Blue. During Desert Storm, the combat troops passed through our city on the way to their Army Stations. For days, the radio would announce when the next troops were coming through and our family, with the kids in tow, would entourage down to Interstate 75 to wave American Flags as the convoy passed by. We affectionately named this activity "The Combat Parade." It was the first introduction the kids had to real live patriotism in their home town and it stuck. To this day, we are a family who still gets cold chills at the singing of "God Bless America" or "The National Anthem". We act upon the compulsion to tell a soldier "thank you" when we see one on the street or at the airport. When 9/11 struck our country, our family mourned and prayed and our kids understood the degree to which this horror struck because of their patriotic upbringing. To this day, Memorial Day and July 4th are monumental celebrations and mandatory attire is America inspired. The one wardrobe rule that the Lt. Colonel stipulates is that "the flag is to be flown, not worn." My children don't stick to that one very well; they can be easily spotted in the "flag" bathing suits! I'm sorry; they love all things America. The story is often told on Chase that when he was young, he hated to spend the night away from home. When he stayed at his Paternal Grandparent's house, he would always sneak into a room after everybody was gone to bed and call me and his dad to come and get him (which we always did). The problem was that his grandparents would wake up in the morning and he was missing! Scared to death, they were! One night, they caught him with the phone – red handed! His grandfather told him to "hang up that phone and get in the bed! You're not calling your mother!" To which Chase replied, "I'm just calling to tell her

'I'm proud to be an American'!" Well you know that stuck! We've even had "Proud to be an American" printed on 4th of July T-shirts!

4th of July Meal
(Repeated at Labor Day)
Lemon Curd Pepper Chicken
Baked Shrimp
Grilled Ribs
Potato Salad
Baked Beans
Watermelon
Slaw
French Bread
Sweet Tea
Homemade Ice Cream and Cookies

Another monumental (although not joyous) occasion in our family occurred in July. Our beloved brother, son, husband, father, and Uncle Chuck was taken from us. Chuck was electrocuted putting the heat and air conditioning unit in Cathy's house. As we later learned, the motor that he used to charge the unit was faulty and he was electrocuted when he picked it up. He was 41 years old and was gone too soon. Chuck was a great son, a great brother, and a great provider for his wife and children. He was a deacon in our church, a Sunday school teacher, and the funniest person I ever knew. He had a wit and a way about him that came out when he didn't even know he was being funny. One story that we love about Chuck is when he went to work for a heating and air company where the boss was a Christian man and advocated prayer for the employees to start off their week. On Chuck's first day there, the boss introduced him, and asked the employees (office workers, repair men, salesmen – the whole crew) to gather around for their usual Monday morning prayer ritual. Chuck, having grown up in our family where when we gather round we hold hands, reached for the fellow's hand next to him and held it while the boss lead in prayer. When the "Amen" was said, Chuck opened his eyes to see every eye on him in a strange way. It was then that he realized that he was the only one that reached out for a hand! The poor fellow next to him never came within ten feet of him again! When he left that employer, it was to be the owner of his own heating and air company. This was a leap of faith for him and his family, but it was also a dream come true. Over the years, Daddy helped him out at the "shop" from time to time when it was busy season. Chuck hired Mark when he was between jobs one summer as well. They saw a side to Chuck while working with him that we wouldn't have known if they hadn't had that opportunity. They got to hear his employees say great things about him. They got to see how he handled conflict in a diplomatic and fair manner. But where we learned the most beautiful things about Chuck was from the hundreds of people that waited in line over three hours to express their condolences to our family when he passed away. We heard tale after tale from people who told about how Chuck had brought them an air conditioner window unit and put it in their house knowing that they couldn't afford to pay for it. He told them, "Don't worry about it – I know things are hard for you." We heard from people who would send in $5 a month on their bill and after a while he called them and said their bill was paid and they didn't owe anymore – when they knew they did. We heard from former employees that said that Chuck had had to let them go for one reason or another but, that he called them from time to time to see how they were doing. One employee told us that Chuck had witnessed to him and changed his life and without having known him, he felt sure he wouldn't be around. Chuck never told us those things. I highlighted in my Bible Matthew 6:1-4 because it reminds me of the way Chuck lived. Verses 3- 4 of The Living Bible say, "When you do a kindness to someone, do it secretly...and your Father who knows all secrets will reward you." He did his good deeds because he had a huge heart; however, I'm sure his heavenly reward was just as huge. Not a day goes by that we don't miss him. Sometimes I still can't believe he's gone. But he left behind a beautiful wife who did a wonderful job raising their children. Tyler and Krista have grown up to be beautiful, caring, loving, Christian young people of whom their dad would be so proud. Tyler once said, "Every happy occasion is met with a little bit of sadness because Dad's not here to share it." I believe the gates of Heaven have been opened up to Chuck from time to time so that he could be a part of Tyler's and Krista's high school graduation, college graduation, wedding day, and the birth of his first grandson. We feel him with us, we remember him, we love him, and we will always miss him!

July Lunch #1
Milanese Chicken
Baked Potatoes
Squash Casserole
Apricot Casserole
Congealed Salad
Rolls
Sweet Tea
Strawberry Shortcake Cake

July Lunch #2
Mediterranean Chicken Breast and Wild Rice
Roasted Vegetables
Blueberry Congealed Salad
Sour Cream Rolls
Sweet Tea
Chocolate Pecan Pie

Josh and Meredith became the proud parents of William Allen Robbs in July. Stella became a big sister, Cappy and Papa Larry became grandparents again, and Gran and Gaca became Great Grandparents for the second time. Little Will has blessed us beyond measure with his always happy disposition and his willingness to go to whoever holds their arms out for him. When Will arrives at Sunday Lunch, he gets passed around sixteen different ways as we are all eager to love on that baby! He doesn't quite make it till the end of lunch before he has fallen asleep in whatever lap he has landed in. Bless his heart. He has no idea how much he is loved.

July Lunch #3
London Broil
Mashed Potatoes
Corn Casserole
Glazed Carrots
Slaw
Sliced Tomatoes
Sweet Tea
Strawberry Pie with Whipped Topping

July Lunch #4
Crock Pot Orange Chicken
Long Grain and Wild Rice
Green Beans
Mixed Vegetable Casserole
Cantaloupe and Watermelon
Rolls
Sweet Tea
Key Lime Pie

AUGUST

August is the time of year when we try to savor the last bits of summer that we can. It is also the month of Dad's birthday as well as when the fifth grandchild, Kaitlin, was born. Daddy's birthday has usually been a cookout complete with homemade ice cream served with his birthday cake. Sometimes he opts for an indoor type meal; but the homemade ice cream never changes! Daddy's wisdom might only be surpassed by his sense of humor. I'd venture to say he is a study in quips. One of my favorites is, when asked how he's doing, Daddy replies, "I'm in good shape for the shape I'm in!" We have all been advised by him that "if you play with skunks, you'll smell just like 'em." A particular quip he used on me when I was a teenager has been the basis of a lot of mimics and hashing about over the years. As a teenager, I did not like to babysit; however, our next door neighbor asked me to babysit about once a week and I had to do it. (Let me take this opportunity to insert another Daddy quip right quick: he said I was gonna babysit and I was gonna enjoy it whether I liked it or not). Anyway, one particular night I was called upon to babysit and I put up a bigger than usual stink about it. Mom told me, "I'm gonna tell your Daddy how you're acting when he gets home" and she did. So by the time I got home from next door, I was in trouble. Daddy sent me to my room and came in there to talk to me and apparently I smarted off to him because he poked his finger in my chest, and quipped to me, "Listen here, little lady. You're up on your high horse and you've picked the wrong night to strut!" Well, my goodness, I got tickled! I couldn't help it. That was the funniest analogy I'd ever heard and I got a spanking that night and I do believe it was because I laughed at his quip more than because I had a smart mouth! That being said, there is something that my Daddy says that was introduced to him by a good friend. In times of sadness, or even times of uncertainty, Daddy says, "Cheer up, hon, the roses will bloom again" and he's always right. Our Daddy is a gentle giant. His stature is big, his heart is big, his mind overflows with wisdom, his humor is limitless, and when he looks at you, shakes that thumb at you (instead of pointing with an index finger) and smiles and says, "I believe everything's gonna be just fine," bank on it – it's gonna be alright. Daddy has always been a hands-on dad to us. He has always provided for us financially, emotionally, and spiritually. He has always been involved in all of our lives. Not only did he always come to every event in which Cathy, Chuck, or I participated, he hasn't missed a sporting event, school program, or graduation of any of the grandchildren either. We know our Dad, our Gaca, is always gonna be there for us. He's always going to root us on and he's always going to make sure we know that he is proud of us. He has never put himself first and has never wanted anything as much as he wants what makes the rest of us happy. It's not unusual that when Daddy is asked what kind of cake he wants for his birthday, his reply is usually, "I believe I'll have whatever you feel like making."

<u>August Lunch #1</u>
Daddy's Birthday Meal
Roast Beef - Sliced
Mashed Potatoes
Broccoli Casserole
Grilled Corn on the Cob
Slaw
Rolls
Sweet Tea
Yellow Cake with Chocolate Icing
Homemade Ice Cream

Mark and I welcomed our second child, Kaitlin, at the end of August. She is the fifth grandchild to be born and the first girl after the four boys. What a change of events when a baby girl came on the scene. She was named in honor of her Aunt Sister, Cathy, and from the moment she arrived, the world was painted pink. She wore pink everything and even though she had no hair, I put a bow on her head by affixing it with a dab of toothpaste. The grandsons treated her like a doll and she reveled in the attention they lavished upon her, but make no mistake, she could hold her own with them. They are probably the reason why she excels at being both a girly girl and an athlete! She has always been very literal; she comes out with what we call "Kaiti-isms". For example, one time her Gran was coming down to the pool with her at Oceans East and when they got in the elevator Kaitlin grabbed her Gran by the arm and said they had to get off that elevator FAST! She said, "Didn't you see the sign, 'Do not use in case of fire'? If it might catch on fire, we don't need to be in it." Despite all Gran's best explanations, they had to take the steps, in case of fire on the elevator. She was and is our resident Amelia Bedelia. One time she heard her paternal grandmother say that she had "carried" her friend, Mozelle, to the store that morning and Kaitlin looked up at her and said, "No, you didn't. You drove her there in the car!" See what I mean? There used to be a commercial on TV encouraging people that "if you just can't take it anymore and need help, call 1-800-867-2421 because we have answers". Well, one day when she was about six years old, Kaitlin came in the kitchen and picked up the phone and started dialing. I said "Wait, wait, wait – who are you calling?" She said, "I'm calling 1-800-867-2421 because Andrew (classmate) keeps aggravating me and I just can't take it anymore and I need help." Oh how I wished someone had been there to share that with me! God love her. As she grew older, her "unique" outlook coupled with her undisputable sanguine personality has served to be some good entertainment at Sunday Lunch.

Gran's typical creation for Kaitlin's birthday cake was a Barbie cake. She made a layer cake, cut a hole down the middle just big enough to hold a Barbie Doll (one she had taken Kaitlin to pick out at Toys R Us, of course) and then the finishing touch would be a satin "skirt" that she would sew and drape around the cake; therefore, it looked like Barbie in a hooped-style evening gown. To cut the cake, the skirt would have to be removed, which was traumatic to the birthday girl, but it was always worth the trade. The cakes evolved into more age appropriate designs over the years, like a flower with each petal a different color, or a softball; however, the cake still remains – red velvet with cream cheese icing. Being born at the end of August, Kaitlin always has outdoor themed birthday meals.

Kaitlin's Birthday Meal
Hamburgers and Turkey Burgers on the grill
Burger Fixings bar:
Lettuce, tomato, onion, pickles, pimento cheese, jalapenos, mayo, mustard, ketchup,
Sweet Baby Rays honey Bar B Q sauce and anything else requested)
Baked Beans
Chips
Sweet Tea
Red Velvet Cake and ice cream

August Lunch # 2
Grilled Bar B Q Chicken
Grilled Corn on the cob
Baked Beans
Texas Toast
Slaw
Sweet Tea
Banana Pudding Pie

August Lunch #3
Lemon Pepper Shrimp Scampi
Salad
Ciabatta Bread
Sweet Tea
Simple Cheesecake

Tyler and Amber gave our family little Wyatt Watson Gross in August. Amber has always been very intent in wanting to know family history and when it was revealed that their baby was to be a boy, she was so happy that the Gross name would continue. Chuck's given name was Wylie Watson Gross, III. So, when it was revealed that Wyatt would also have the initials of WWG, we as a family were touched beyond measure. Having been born one month apart, Will and Wyatt will know what it's like to grow up

56

cousin friends just like their parents did. Wyatt is the spitting image of his daddy with the way he is content to take it all in. He is happy and quiet and eager to go to whatever arms reach for him. We are so blessed to have these additions to our family. It's very rewarding to look at our kids and see them be the parents we always hoped they would be. As our family grows, the foundation of it gets stronger and stronger.

<u>August Lunch #4</u>
Chicken Enchiladas
Corn
Black Beans
Tostito Chips
Salsa
Chocolate Fudge Cake and ice cream

SEPTEMBER

The South is known for a lot of things, but because we are in the upper South, the colors of the fall are some of the most beautiful sights you can imagine. However, the leaves on the trees are not the only things that change in the fall for our family. Our palates change from peaches to pumpkin. We love some cobbler in this group and the cooler weather brings on an appetite for all things warm that can be topped with a little brown sugar or ice cream (both if you can get by with it). September celebrations include mine and Jordan's birthday. Now, I have to enlighten you that September is also the month in which we all try to adjust to a new schedule, what with school back in session and all. See, Aunt Sister taught school for 30 years and her body clock starts winding down at about 8:30pm, and it just wears the rest of us out. She starts rubbing that make up off her eyes, about 8:30 and by 8:45, she's in a full blown sneezing fit. I am not exaggerating. Much. Because of her body clock, we had to move Family Movie Night to Friday or Saturday in the fall (instead of our customary Sunday night in the summer). When Cathy and I lived in the same neighborhood, we gathered for movie night at her house one night a week. Some of the movies that were chosen were at the suggestion of the boys, or just a random pick at Blockbuster. We gathered on her sectional sofa, and each of us had our own blanket and by the time the movie was over, those who were still awake often found themselves buried under a sleeping child or nephew on either shoulder/lap. There was, on occasion, screaming that could be heard city-wide. The one distinguishable yell belonged to Mark, who would scream like a woman at the unexpected horror on the screen. Jordan was known to get hungry half way through (although we had consumed multiple bags of microwave popcorn in the community bowl) and he would inevitably be rattling around in a bag of chips and popping a can of Dr. Pepper to which Mark would announce, "Pause the movie!! Jordan, get that bag opened and get it quiet!" It was all in good humor, of course, but that moment of interruption seemed to cause a bladder attack in everybody in which we had to unfold off that couch, get relief, and then try to recreate our previous comfort pile. Of course, Kaitlin had long ago crawled up in Cathy's "big bed" and gone to sleep and Cathy would just join her there later. There were times, when the movie was a dud and I fully admit to walking back home in my pajamas and robe but only with Cathy standing on her front porch to make sure I got home (four doors up). I've never been known for anything as much as a chicken. One time, after a really scary movie, Mark and I actually had to deliberate whether we were walking home or spending the night at Sister's. Turns out we weren't the only ones who got scared. One night the boys were all at Cathy's house (which was often the case) and they called Mark and me absolutely all yelling at the same time and scared to death. They had been arguing amongst each other and had gone into Cathy's room for her to be the moderator. All of the sudden the door closed to her room and they just knew they clearly saw the shadow of feet walk by under the door. They were calling us and wanting us to know that they knew it was Mark who had come down there and walked by the door and shut it! Uh, no, we're too scared to walk home – why would we scare somebody else? Those boys will swear and declare to this day that somebody walked past the door and they just know it was Mark. I can assure you it wasn't and I think they know that, too, but it brings them comfort to think it was! It's always an adventure looking for a place to happen when this group gathers together.

<u>September Lunch #1</u>
Chicken Divan
Rice
Shoepeg Corn
Mom's Frozen Fruit Salad
Sour Cream Rolls
Sweet Tea
Cherry Crisp and ice cream

Since my birthday is in the middle of the month, I'm always excited to break out something "fall" to wear to my own party and, typically, my birthday falls around the time the new fall lineup starts on TV. So, in my younger days, I remember the excitement I felt for the new season of some of the BEST shows that were ever on television. *The Brady Bunch, Lucy, Family Affair*, and *That Girl* were some of my favorites! On Saturdays, Cathy, Chuck and I watched *American Bandstand*; Saturday night the whole family watched *Hee Haw* followed by *The Ed Sullivan Show* and Mom made homemade hamburgers in the skillet. Sunday night, after church, we watched *Bonanza* and had Sunday night sandwiches like egg salad, tuna salad, or roast beef left over from Sunday Lunch. I'll add this little nugget: one of the biggest shows was *Bewitched*; however, Saint Mary could not abide by that nose twitching "magic" and we weren't free to indulge in that TV show unless 1) she reluctantly allowed it "this one time" or 2) we were home sick from school (in which we could only watch TV if we had a fever). That Saint Mary ran a tight ship, didn't she? Growing up, Mom had a recipe for roast beef that included mushroom soup and I called it mushroom meat. It was always my go-to for my birthday meal. As I got older and the family got bigger, I opted for grilled chicken because a) it went further and b) I was always trying to keep it diet friendly. (Actually I could count the weight watcher points for chicken and trying to figure out the mushroom meat was impossible). So, with a tablescape of blue toile tablecloth, blue candles, and the Blue Willow china, and fresh yellow flowers, I was surrounded by my favorite colors, my favorite food, fall clothes waiting to be unwrapped, and my family. This was my beginning of a Happy Fall Ya'll!

September Lunch #2
Lori's Birthday Menu
Mushroom Meat
Mashed Potatoes
Green Bean Casserole
Cathy's Strawberry Pretzel Salad
Macaroni and Cheese
Rolls

German Chocolate Cake or
Italian Cream Cake

Jordan is the fourth grandchild born, as well as the third grandchild born in the year 1985. Our knowledge that Cathy was expecting another child came at the birth of Chase. When a birth is happening, the whole family turns out in the waiting room! We don't come when the mother is eight centimeters. We go when she goes. So, when Chase was born in January, and I had gotten settled in my hospital room, I wondered why the only person that hadn't come to see me was my sister. I knew she was there because I saw her throughout labor and when the family got to see the baby. So when I asked where she was, my Daddy said, "Well, Sis, I hate to worry you, but she passed out in the waiting room and the Doctor wanted to admit her for observation. So, she's in a room down the hall." Turns out, what they had "observed" was that Sister was with child! Later on, when they wheeled her into my room, all we could do was laugh because when in the world do three siblings have babies all in the same year? And the babies are all boys? What a blessing!

Jordan can best be described as laid back, adaptable, and basically just proud to be here. He is adventurous, mischievous, and as loving as anybody you could ever meet. He is never met without a hug or left without an "I love you." In his younger days, it was not uncommon for Jordan to come in the house with a treasure he found – usually one he had dug up from the ground. Alive. Moving. Bless his heart. He loved any kind of video game and was self-proclaimed "the best in the world at Tiger Woods Golf in 2005!" Jordy is creative in every way. He can take a piece of wood and turn it into a table just figuring it out as he goes. He has helped Gaca out many times painting, doing kitchen remodeling, putting up a wall, whatever needs to be done. One thing you'll always hear Jordan say when he's leaving Sunday Lunch is, "Call me if you need anything!" God's perfect mate for him is his beautiful bride Kristen. As an Interior Design major, she is just as creative as Jordan and together, they make an incredible team. Like all the boys, Jordan is a sports lover. For some reason, from the time he was a little boy Jordan's cake usually represented the Pittsburg Steelers. He plugged into the Steelers early on and he has always been a fan! To see that Steeler logo painted on a football field on a birthday cake would make anybody a fan! Like Tyler, Jordan had a dinosaur cake one year, but he went back to the Steelers year after year. As he got older, the cake became a layer cake; but, that Steeler logo remained.

<u>September Lunch #3</u>
Jordan's Birthday Meal
Robbs Family Recipe Spaghetti
Salad with Balsamic Vinaigrette
French Bread with Oil/Spices for dipping
Birthday cake with homemade icing

<u>September Lunch #4</u>
Chicken Pot Pie
Baked Potato
Pears with mayonnaise and shredded cheese
Crescent Rolls
Sweet Tea
Brabson House Cajun Cake

OCTOBER

Now, I'm sure nobody would be surprised to know that even though our family does not celebrate witches and ghosts, we do put together a shin dig for Halloween in the form of good old fashioned pumpkins, scarecrows, and Sam. Sam is a "man" that Gaca created one year that sits on their front porch on Halloween. He is created out of newspaper-stuffed blue overalls, a pumpkin head covered with a straw hat, and he holds a rake. He wears big ole work boots and looks a little creepy, not gonna lie. When the kids were younger, Halloween night always included a trip to Gran and Gaca's to trick or treat after the neighborhood round had been exhausted. Now, I'll remind you that Chase didn't do well with totem poles and Polynesian people and he sure didn't do well with Sam. So convincing him to stand by Sam for a photo op was not always successful until he was completely convinced Sam couldn't move! In later years, Sam was moved to the living room and welcomed us all at the Sunday Lunch closest to Halloween. To this day, there are treat bags for all from Gran and Gaca which includes each person's favorite candy, gum, and always a bit of money for the kids. Each bag has our name on it with a Halloween sticker of a pumpkin, or harvest, or some God-created thing – never a witch or a ghost or a bat (because at Halloween, bats are evil, says St. Mary).

October is also the time when Aunt Sister gets her Christmas shopping britches on. Inevitably, one Sunday in October, she'll pull out that infernal notebook and pass around a sheet with everybody's name on it. We are instructed to put our "wish list" for Christmas on that page which includes our sizes, the colors we like, what gift cards we prefer, the stocking stuffers we love, and, of course, we are free to put down what we DON'T want or need. It is a huge help; but, bless that Aunt Sister's heart, she loves to have us filling out lists – from New Year's Resolutions, to Christmas lists, and even Personality Profiles...we are an organized bunch if nothing else. By October, we have also polled the family to see what they'd like to have for the upcoming Sunday Lunches. We like to get input on the favorites and with sweet potato and pumpkin everything coming up, we like to put in variety every chance we get.

October Lunch #1
Pork Tenderloin
Town and Country Sweet Potatoes
Green Peas
Corn Casserole
Slaw
Biscuits
Sweet Tea
Pumpkin Crunch Dessert

October Lunch #2
Meat Loaf
Mashed Potatoes
Pinto Beans
Stewed Tomatoes
Macaroni and Cheese
Fried Okra
Slaw Cornbread
Sweet Tea
Banana Pudding

October Lunch #3
Poppyseed Chicken
Baked Potatoes
Green Beans
Congealed Salad
Garlic Biscuits
Sweet Tea
Pumpkin Cheese Cake

October Lunch #4
Pot Roast with Potatoes, Carrots, Onions
Silver Queen Corn
Green Bean Almandine
Slaw
Apple Cobbler with ice cream

NOVEMBER

It was never in question that our family believed in prayer and we knew from an early age the importance of it. Each one of us kids accepted Jesus as our savior by the age of seven and we knew exactly how that commitment would forever impact our lives. Our parents led by example and we knew that God was the center of our home. When our church decided to move locations, we knew that the building in which all of us had been baptized would be torn down. Chuck surprised us all the following Christmas by giving each of us a framed stained glass window pane from the old church with an inscription on it of the date we made our professions of faith. It hangs prominently in each of our homes and serves as a vivid reminder of our conversion experience and of the way Chuck loved us and our memories of Dodds Ave. enough to preserve a part of them for us forever. If it's true that the family that prays together stays together, then we should be bound up pretty tight. There have been those occasions over the years where praying got taken to a level beyond bowed head and folded hands. I remember when I was about ten years old, my Daddy had his pilot's license and he traveled for his job to various shopping centers that the company he worked for was building around the southeast. One night, Daddy was supposed to be home at his usual time of 5:30 p.m. and he wasn't home yet. Well, Mom started getting all nervous in that looking –out-the-window –trance-like state at about 5:50. He wasn't usually anything so much as prompt. But on this night, it was 8:00 and Mom had regressed to the crying-head-bowed-hand-wringing state when we couldn't find anybody to give us any information on where he was. It had already been decided by Mom by about 6:00 that he'd "gone off in that airplane and crashed somewhere" (although at ten years old, I was fairly certain that would have been on the news). We were downstairs at Daddy's desk looking through every paper we could find for another contact number when he walked through that door at 9:00 p.m. After the initial hollering of "Thank you, Lord Jesus, he's here! Oh Lordy! Thank you, Jesus" by mom, the rest of us had run to Daddy while we cried "I'm so glad to see you!" Daddy looked absolutely verklempt over all the carrying on! So after Mom recovered from her hysteria she got up off that floor where she had hit her knees to pray and she looked at Daddy and said, in the clearest, non-crying, non-hysterical voice you ever heard and said "Wylie! Where have you been? I thought you were dead! I've called every hospital looking for you!" She was mad as a hornet. He said, "Well, Mary, I told you this morning I had to go to Arkansas and I'd be late getting home" to which Mom replied (after what seemed like an hour) "Well.........I forgot."

Another time that I remember hollered out prayers was when Cathy, Chuck, and I had a pillow fight while Mom and Dad had gone out for a walk. It was all impromptu as we had never done this before and I can assure you we never did it again. (The other first and only was the fact that Mom and Dad went out for a walk! That only happened on this one night, too!) When Chuck lived at home, our den off the kitchen was divided into two rooms in order to make one room a bedroom for Chuck. The other room became a study. It had one wall of bookshelves that housed more books than the public library (that's a hyperbole). In the middle of the bookshelves was a very large aquarium that was the pride of the house. For some reason, just after mom and dad left for their walk, somebody threw a pillow at somebody. Somebody threw one back. A full blown pillow fight erupted and don't you know one of those pillows burst wide open and feathers went EVERYWHERE!!! I mean in between books, inside lamps, floating in the aquarium, in the curtains and the valance – listen to me – EVERYWHERE!!! We froze!! And without saying a word we scattered six ways to Sunday and each of us came back with a cleaning utensil of some kind. Here's the thing – Mama kept that house like the Queen of England was coming and we were sure on this particular night she was due any minute. In utter fear and calling upon the name of Jesus in ways that differed from the ordinary prayer-like address, we set in to cleaning that mess. The first words that were uttered were from Cathy and they were "Oh dear Lord!! Here they come!" About the time the downstairs door closed, we put away the last cleaning tool – under the couch. We all agreed it looked just as good as it did when they'd left and the last thing I remember before the door to the study opened was Cathy saying "Just act normal!" (Really?) When mom walked in that room she was a-gasp and said, "What in the world have you done to this room?" We were flabbergasted! Of course, we said, "Nothing?" in unison, by the way. Mom exclaimed, "Well, for doing nothing, there sure are a lot of feathers in this room!! I have cleaned all day long!" We looked around like the innocent children we were not and said, "Where?" to which there was a resounding "There are feathers in Lori's braids, not to mention the windows and lamp shades." Busted. Of course, the three of us got tickled but didn't dare laugh, Daddy scooted on off and Mom told us to "Go on! All of you!" and she cleaned it herself. We all laughed about it....eventually! To this day Mom says that night held one of her big regrets because she didn't just laugh. It's ok, Mom; I'm sure it wasn't funny at the time. You've made up for it because we have laughed plenty over it since. The look on your face when you saw that room was priceless!

<u>November Lunch #1</u>
Chicken with Dried Beef
Baked Potatoes
Peas
Carrot Soufflé
Broccoli Cole Slaw
Crescent Rolls
Sweet Tea
Glazed Apple Crumb Cake

<u>November Lunch #2</u>
Sausage Pinwheels
White Beans
Stewed Tomatoes
Fried Okra
Chow Chow
Cornbread
Sweet Tea
Apple Pie a la Mode

November Lunch #3
Beef Shepherd's Pie
Turkey Shepherd's Pie
Salad
Sweet Tea
Cherry Crunch with Ice Cream

November Lunch #4
Spanish Spaghetti with Olives
Tossed Salad
Focaccia Bread
Sweet Tea
Chocolate Chip Pound Cake with Ice Cream

So not only do we understand prayer, we understand "Thankful"! People, we do thankful every day! Because we have suffered disease, we are thankful for our health. Because we have suffered death, we are thankful for life. Because we have suffered unemployment, we are thankful for our jobs. Because we have suffered through everything together, we are thankful for our family. Because our parents taught us the meaning of sacrifice and that nothing is too big or too small to take to the Lord in prayer, we are a family that has seen first-hand the power of prayer and that if we want to make sure that "all things work together for the good for those who love God and are called according his purpose" (Romans 8:28), then we know the necessity of giving thanks in all things. So when we come together as a family on Thanksgiving, it's a humbling time for us to reminisce over the past year and truly give thanks for our blessings.

We gather at Gran and Gaca's for Thanksgiving for the evening meal and we are met with a tablescape that embodies all things Thanksgiving. It has fruit, nuts, and, foliage, all spilling out from cornucopias. There are pilgrim figurines on each end and all of this is on a mirror that runs down the center of the table. With other fluffs added, such as gold netting, taper candles, votives, and small pumpkins, it is truly a beautiful representation of a bountiful harvest. Just before dinner, we gather together in the den where Gran has prepared scripture verses regarding being thankful on strips of paper – one for each of us. We go around the room and read the scripture and then tell of what we are thankful for over the last year. As we have gotten older, our "thankfuls" have evolved into new family members, provisions of health and finances, and, naturally, that after all these years, we are still together. At the time of this writing, Gaca turned 88 in August and Gran will be 90 in December. We as a family are so grateful that God has allowed us all to experience so much life, together. Cathy and I are so thankful to have our parents for all these years; the grandchildren realize how blessed they are to have grandparents still with them. We know that the lessons we have learned about living, and loving, and laughing together as a family is a gift bestowed upon us by God and we are more than thankful! Ironically our parents were married in the month of November, Thanksgiving weekend in 1949.

Thanksgiving
Turkey
Cornbread Dressing
Gravy
Mashed Potatoes
Broccoli Casserole
Sweet Potato Casserole
Corn Pudding
Green Bean Casserole – Chase's
Cranberry Relish
Homemade Rolls
Sweet Tea
Pecan Pie
Pumpkin Pie

DECEMBER

December is such a blessed month! Not only do we celebrate with full festivities the birth of Jesus; but, we also celebrate Mom's birthday and Krista's birthday. Not that anyone's birth is any less miraculous than another's; but, Krista's birth is truly a miracle, and just a pure-de-ole tale that is best told in person because, I'll admit, it's best told when I can act out the scenes, just a tad. Krista is the sixth grandchild born to Gran and Gaca, being born just three months after Kaitlin; they are bonded like sisters more than cousins. Since Mark and I lived within five miles of Chuck and Teresa, we had a plan in place that when Teresa went into labor, we would come and get Tyler so that they could head on to the hospital. Early one morning, about 6:15, Chuck called and asked me, a little suspiciously, I might add, what kind of symptoms I felt when I had gone into labor with Kaitlin. I can attest from working in an OB/Gyn office, as well as having birthed two babies nearly four years apart, every labor is different and it's hard to remember how labor feels from one child to the next. He asked me a few questions that prompted me to tell him I thought it would be a good idea to call the doctor and let him know what was going on. He said he would do that and we hung up. About ten minutes later, I got another phone call from my brother, who, when I answered the phone was speaking in a higher than normal pitch, and a little "excited" sounding said, "Uh, Lori, this is Chuck? Teresa's having this baby? At home? I need you to come get Tyler now? I've called an ambulance but they're not here. Can you hurry?" LORDHAVEMERCY! I had Kaitlin in the bed with me feeding her at the time and I jumped up, gave her to Mark, opened my closet and put on the first shoes I found which were hot pink, ran out the door hollering back to Mark what was going on and I headed out to Chuck's house in my pink gown, hot pink shoes, no coat, and ice on the road, driving my straight shift Honda Civic. I heard sirens the whole way but I couldn't see any emergency vehicles! I was calling out to Jesus: "Oh Lord! Get me there before the ambulance!! Just get me there!" I had a visual of Tyler sitting on the curb and Chuck and Teresa gone to the hospital. But, when I pulled up, what I found was Chuck walking back and forth across the front yard, rubbing that mustache and there I was, jumping out the car before I let the clutch off and banging my head about five times on the door frame trying to get out of it! I said "I hear the sirens" and Chuck said "I hear 'em!! Where are they?" I said, "Where's Teresa?" and Chuck said, "Upstairs in the bathroom!" Mind you, these questions were being hollered in a panic kind of hollering! I said "Then, what are you doing down here?" I set off in a sprint inside that house and the first thing I heard coming from upstairs was an unmistakable yell from a woman in labor! Their staircase was one in which halfway up was a landing that took a 45 degree turn before heading up the next set of steps. As I took those stairs two at a time, I looked straight ahead at the top step and there was Teresa in the bathroom in pure agony!! I ran in there and right away I saw that the baby had crowned and we were fixing to do some work! I got her in the floor and she was as compliant as anything I've ever seen because, I reckon in that condition, you'll do whatever you're told. I opened the linen closet and got a stack of towels and put them under her rump to prop her up a bit and in my calmest, confident, yet commanding voice (folks, it was all Holy Spirit-lead because me by myself would have been a match shy of an explosion at this point) I explained to Teresa that we were fixin' to have a baby and that everything was going to be ok and for her to just do what I directed her to do. Here's the scene going on in the adjacent bedroom: Tyler, at almost four years old, was sitting straight up in his mom and dad's bed, looking straight ahead, and not moving! Chuck, who was still pacing between window and bedroom and hallway, was still rubbing that mustache and saying, over and over, "Oh, sweet Jesus, come and help me. Oh, sweet Jesus!" I gently suggested to him, "Chuck, why don't you call 911 back and see where they are?" I wanted to say dammit but I didn't. Forgive me, Lord. So, while Chuck is on the phone with 911, I hear him say, in that still high pitched voice that he usually didn't possess, "Uh, hello, Operator? This is Chuck Gross and I called a little while ago because my wife is having a baby? Here? At home? And no one is here yet?" Meanwhile, back in the hallway with the birth mother, I was directing her that on my

71

count to three, she was going to bear down and push. So, having just done this three months earlier, it was fresh on my mind what real live labor nurses and a real live obstetrician had instructed me to do. By the grace of God, those instructions came out of my mouth to Teresa. But here's the thing – one push and that baby was coming out! So, I very calmly but loud enough for him to hear, let's just say – I called out to Chuck and said "IT'S HERE!". To which he relayed to the 911 operator, "Never, mind, operator, they're here!" and he hung up! HE HUNG UP THE PHONE!! I really "called out" this time and I said, "NOT THEM!!! THE BABY!!"   I'm telling you the God's honest truth we were starting to look like Archie and Edith Bunker and I'm the one being Archie! So, let's review. Teresa's in the floor, I'm in position, delivering a baby, Chuck has joined us by her side, rubbing her head and pushing her hair back, saying (crying), "I love you, Babe. I love you so much." Tyler is still in the middle of the bed (out of eyesight) when low and behold up that second set of steps appears Gaca, followed by Gran! Could it get anymore unreal?! Because Chuck had called them, after he called me, they thought they would drive by the house on the way to the hospital. But seeing cars still there, they, like me, thought they were coming into a situation where an inevitable trip to the hospital was going to be made and it just hadn't happened yet. So, Gaca looks up, sees the Lifetime movie taking place right in front of him and simply says "Oh. Scuse me," turns about face and heads back down the steps while I'm spouting off "Mom, get Tyler out of the bedroom!" She doesn't miss a beat, darts in that room, sweeps Tyler up in her arms and has his little head buried and covered and scoots down those steps as fast as anything I've ever seen. Understand that all this is happening simultaneously with a birth going on and the birth mother coming thru like a champ! In my mind, I was praying, "Lord, please let this baby be breathing, let this baby cry, let this be ok!" So, just as Gran disappears around that landing, another push sends that baby right out into this world! Never before and never since have I so clearly witnessed the hand of God right in front of my eyes. That precious angel came into this world, face down, looked up, and without any stimulation but the hand of God, she cried! It was the audible voice of God saying

"She's perfect. She's healthy. I've got this!" We all three were crying and rejoicing and when I told them it was a girl, we squealed and Chuck rubbed Teresa's head till I thought it would be raw and he kept saying a combo of "Oh, thank you, sweet Jesus" and "I love you so much, Babe." And then – the Paramedics arrived! There we were in that hallway, with the daddy kissing the momma on the head, the "midwife" in a pink nursing gown and hot pink shoes, and Mr. Fireman First Responder thinking HE was in charge. He tore up on that scene thinking he was gonna deliver a baby or something and immediately started shouting out orders! "Get Daddy out of here!" he demanded. "Everybody calm down and clear out!" he further demanded. I'm here to tell you the Archie Bunker in me quickly became one demon shy of Lucifer and as I'm sitting on my knees with a baby fresh out the birth canal and in my towel wrapped arms, I looked up at Sergeant Late for the Party and with all the fire I could muster up I informed him "No sir. Daddy ain't going nowhere, everybody IS calm but YOU and the delivered baby is right here in my hand!" You talk about a change of attitude – Late for the Party looked like he'd had a bucket of cold water thrown on his superiority and he back peddled real fast. He stepped, as delicate as was possible in a fireman's coat and fireman boots, over the bodies in the floor, scooted up behind me, and instructed that on his count he would slide his arms under mine and we would transfer the baby to him to complete the process. I might add, he was very complimentary of how we had handled everything without the help of professionals. I refrained from informing him that there are some things that have nothing to do with professionals as much as it does with not being able to stop a train. That baby was coming with or without a "professional." However, once the "professional" took over, he was kind and comforting and attended to the rest of the details. One of those details was that they wrapped the baby in what looked like aluminum foil to hold in her body heat and placed her on her Momma's belly. When they did that, the first thing out of Chuck's mouth was "Look, Babe. It looks like a Sunday Roast." Is food ever far from our minds? Before it was all said and done, in front of the house were two police cars, an ambulance, a first responder truck, and a ladder truck from the fire department. They loaded up the mother and baby on a gurney and beat up the hallway quite a bit trying to maneuver it down those steps and the landing but eventually, they got to the hospital and made a perfect recovery. Oh what a day! Krista Marie was born shortly before 7:00am – a lot happened between the first 6:15 phone call and the sound of that little baby crying. My sweet brother called me two hours later and when I answered the phone he said "Lori? Thank you! I love you! I don't know what else to say but that I can't believe all that just happened!" We both agreed that we had experienced in unmistakable fashion the precious hand of God.

Unlike the way she entered this world, Krista was always the quiet one of the bunch. Now, it's possible that being the sixth grandchild might not have given her much opportunity for input; however, she and Kaitlin always stuck together as the only girls and the quietness was replaced with lots of laughter when the two of them got together! They have always been more like sisters than cousins. As a little girl, Krista often walked around singing songs she learned in Sunday school. We used to tease her and call her "Snoopy" because she liked to unwrap the Christmas presents and see what she was getting and then wrap them back up again – perfectly! As a young woman, she went to the Dominican Republic on mission trips; I keep a picture of her surrounded by her Dominican kids in my Bible and it always makes me smile. It reminds me that I saw God's hand on that precious girl when she was born and I can still see it. Krista met her perfect mate, Adam, and they were recently married. Adam has brought Krista out of her quiet shell – just a tad! Like all the other mates the kids have found, Adam fits our family perfectly. Growing up, Krista also had Barbie doll cakes. Some of her Barbies had blonde hair, some brown but they always had a pink gown! As she grew older, her cakes represented her love of basketball and eventually a layer cake with, of course, pink decorations.

December Lunch #1
Krista's Birthday Meal
Poppyseed Chicken

Baked Potato
Baked asparagus
Salad
Rolls
Sweet Tea
Chocolate Wafer Pie (aka WMU pie)

Gran's birthday falls on the day after Krista's. So even though they celebrate birthdays on consecutive days, they have their own parties! We try very hard to make Gran's birthday as special as possible for the woman who has lived every day putting her family first and making sure all of our celebrations were nothing less than extraordinary. Mom had the toughest job of all- being a stay at home mom. She was always one step ahead of our every need. She cooked, sewed, organized, planned vacations, made sure we felt loved, special, celebrated, and prepared. She got us ready for camp, Brownies, Girl Scouts, church activities, and school. And when we were old enough, she taught us how to do all those things for our own kids. Most of all, Mom is a prayer warrior who leads by example; she epitomizes the Proverbs 31 woman. I remember, as a child, when I was sick, my mom's hand felt so good on me – it was always cool and soft. She would stay in the room with us when we were sick and it felt better just knowing she was there. She would go to the grocery store every Thursday morning. In the summer I would get up early and go with her because, "when momma gets her coat on, Lori gets her coat on." She writes us notes on special days, for sure; but, Mom sends us notes in the mail just to say she loves us or to express her pride in something we have done. Her letters are always signed, "Proud to be, Your Mom" and then she references Philippians 4:13. She does this for the grandchildren, too. She sends them letters and cards any time they have successes or setbacks and she always references Jeremiah 29:11, *For I know the plans I have for you, plans to prosper you and not to harm you,, plans to give you hope and a future.* All of the grandchildren lead successful lives and they all have a committed relationship with the Lord. They will all tell you that their Gran and Gaca have always been there to lift them up in prayer and rejoice in all their accomplishments. All of us siblings had career aspirations and we all attained them. Chuck, an engineer, Cathy, an educator, and me, I wanted to be a wife and mother just like Mom. I will always strive to be the "just like Mom" part – but to be half the mom she is would be my greatest honor. On her 80th birthday we all wrote her a letter regarding what she means to us. We read the letters aloud to her and compiled them in a notebook. This year, we will celebrate her 90th birthday and we will dedicate our memories of *Sunday Lunch* to her in hopes that she will find joy in all the memories she has given us as a family.

Mom's Birthday Meal
Roast Beef
Twice Baked Potatoes
Green Beans
Corn
Slaw
Rolls
Sweet Tea
Hershey's Chocolate Cake

December Lunch #2
Spicy Beef Roast
Smashed parmesan Potatoes
Corn Pudding
Carrot Soufflé
Green Peas
7-layer Salad
Sweet Tea
Chocolate Wafer Pie

December Lunch #3
Mushroom Asiago Chicken
Mashed Potatoes
Roasted Vegetables
Salad
Homemade Italian Bread
Sweet Tea

Red Velvet Cake

December Lunch #4
Crock Pot Italian Dressing Chicken
Brown Rice
Green Beans
Frozen Fruit Salad
Sister Shubert Rolls
Fudge Pie with Ice Cream

Christmas is as traditional and as celebrated as is humanly possible in our family. Throughout the month we have had various Christmas parties what with all the Sunday school class parties, choir parties, caroling, the Family Reunion Christmas party, and add to that all the parties associated with each person's employment. To tell you the truth, we eat from Thanksgiving to New Year's Day. (Then we resolve to not eat like that anymore, which lasts till the next Sunday). Christmas Eve day is spent putting finishing touches on everything from presents to food. Mom always bakes cookies – I mean she bakes all things sweet! There's pecan tassies, pecan crescents, coconut date bars, white chocolate dipped Ritz crackers with peanut butter and a chocolate pound cake. I remember in my younger days helping her make fruit cakes and letting them soak in grape juice while wrapped up in a towel. Of course, no Christmas season would be complete without several batches of Chex Mix and boxes of Whitman's Samplers sitting around. By the time we get to the Christmas Eve Candlelight service, I've had to go over to the Walmart and get a tunic to wear 'cause I've eaten myself out of my clothes. (Side note: Get you a black tent dress; throw on a piece of Christmas jewelry and hang on to it year after year for the Candlelight service. It won't be so obvious you've eaten ten pounds of baked goods in three weeks. Works like a charm.) While Mom bakes for weeks, Daddy puts holiday touches on the outside of the house. He strings lights on the bushes, hangs wreathes on the shutters, buys one live tree for the downstairs, and gets the other decorations out of the attic which includes a Christmas tree for the living room, one for the upstairs den, and one for the sunroom. I'm telling you it's a production! In our own homes, we have taken on the same traditions. All of us deck the halls, bake the goods, and wrap a lot of presents! In each of our homes, we display, all year long, a hand carved manger scene that Chuck brought each of us from the Holy Land. We all find great joy, not just in the beauty of the decorations and Christmas trees; but, we know that we have passed on to our own children the joy of celebrating, the traditions that were instilled in us as kids, and the exceptional blessing of being with family.

Our Christmas Eve service was always a beautiful time to reflect on the birth of Jesus and the love of Christ to send us His only son. We would partake of The Lord's Supper and have various musical contributions from instrumental to choral to soloists. Many years, either Sister or I, or "the Trio" (as Cathy, Teresa, and I were called) were asked to provide a musical selection for the service. One year the Trio was asked to sing "Ring the Bells" as we had about a thousand times before between Sunday school class parties, Sunday morning worship, or during Sunday school department assemblies. Let me say that we were a good trio! Cathy was soprano, Teresa second soprano, and I sang alto. We harmonized beautifully; however, just like at my Aunt Mildred's funeral, sometimes things didn't turn out like we practiced. This one particular service, we were singing "Ring the Bells" and we were on the last phrase of the song where it ends with singing that phrase –Ring The Bells - 3 times. Each time we sang that line was worse than the line before and the pitch was so off on that last "Ring. The. Bells" that we looked something akin to a beagle dog tilting his head and raising one ear. We proceeded to sashay off that stage and instead of going back to our seats, Teresa picked up her full length mink coat off the pew and walked straight out the door! I wanted to high-tale it out right behind her but my polyester sweater was a few rows back and I couldn't get to it fast enough. Cathy and I, once again, sat with heads bowed trying every way in the world to keep it together. Now, the other hundred times we sang, it was fine but, the two that were particularly horrible (Aunt Mildred's Funeral and Christmas Eve) have a way of standing out in your mind; they're the ones you have nightmares over! Anyway, all's well that ends well and the service always ended with singing "Silent Night" by candlelight, acapella. It was beautiful, reverent, and certainly a blessing that it was the memory people left with! When I hear *Silent Night* I always think of Chuck because he used to sit for hours to learn how to play that song on his guitar. He would strum about every other chord right and then when he thought he had it figured out, he'd start trying to sing with it. Oh it was a mess most of the time! But God love him, he worked hard on it and I'd give anything to hear it again. I will...one day. For many years, after the candlelight service, Joan and Nick hosted us at their house for a Holiday Gathering. We would gather in their home with their kids and celebrate Christmas over dinner and games of pool and ping pong in their gorgeous home. Now when I say "dinner", it is the understatement of the decade. Joan puts on a spread! She puts out a kitchen full of southern delicacies that you have to use two plates to get through the serving line because you don't want to pass on a single dish! AND the dining room has a buffet of picturesque desserts. We get to laugh and reminisce about old times and in the process, we make new memories. It is the essence of Holiday Family Fellowship. It is a highlight of the season!

To this day, Christmas morning begins like it did all the years we kids lived at home! Santa comes! Now that we have families of our own, we start Christmas morning early at our individual homes and then gather at Gran and Gaca's by 8:00 am to celebrate together. We start upstairs in the den where we enjoy Gran's LeConte Sunrise punch, breakfast that includes country ham and biscuits among other things and then Gaca reads the Christmas Story from Luke 2. Gran and Gaca go downstairs first and then the rest of us descend one at a time in order of birth and we pause on the last step so Gran can take our picture. The sight is one to behold! Santa has been there and left presents for all nineteen of us! There is a stocking basket full of toiletries and fun extras along with an unwrapped Santa item and wrapped presents as well. The fourteen-seat table is filled with presents for Gran and Gaca! We try to open our gifts one person at a time so we can all see what each other got but, sometimes, it gets a little less organized than that! Each year the blessings become even more priceless because we realize how fortunate we are to still have all but one of us together. We recognize that we have established magnificent memories and timeless traditions, and all the while we have strengthened the foundation of our faith based family. Thank you, Lord, for blessings unmeasurable and unconditional love that binds us as a forever family.

Christmas Breakfast
Cheese Strata
Ham and Biscuits
Sausage and Biscuits
Sausage Balls
Overnight Blueberry French Toast
Fruit
LeConte Sunrise
Orange Juice, Milk, Coffee

In our younger days, Christmas dinner was held at our grandmother's house. As we grew older and so did our grandparents, dinner was at Gran and Gaca's house. It was a traditional affair with Turkey and all the trimmings! About twenty years ago, Cathy started having Christmas dinner at her house. So, after the gift giving and the cleaning up, she would scurry on to her house to get ready for the evening gathering. Sister puts together a tablescape for magazines; I'm telling you what's the truth. It drips in Poinsettias, candles, gold ribbon, her finest China and those Crimson Red Goblets that scream Christmas! The rest of us scurried to the nearest couch for a nap or went to visit with in-laws. We all had our assignments to bring for dinner and at the customary 6:00 the p.m., we once again gathered together for food, fun, and family. We have always reflected on how long we planned for Christmas and the day just flew by! But it has never disappointed, never gone unappreciated, and never left us feeling anything other than blessed.

Christmas Dinner
Turkey/Dressing
Mashed Potatoes
Sweet Potato Casserole
Broccoli Casserole
Cranberry Salad
Homemade rolls
Assorted Baked Goods
Pecan Pie
Pumpkin Pie

Here's the thing. Family is a blessing. Pure and simple. My family has had its share of adversities and blessings, successes and frustrations, grief and happiness – you name it. But what we have also had is the knowledge that there was nothing that we could not get through together. We give each other stability and we truly, truly love and care about each other. I am so grateful to our parents for instilling in us the fact that nothing is more important than each other and that when we keep God in the center of our lives and in the middle of our relationships, He will give us the strength we need when we are weak and the joy we need when we are sad. Romans 12:12 reminds me to "Be joyful in hope, patient in affliction, and faithful in prayer." My mom reminds me when I doubt myself that "I can do all things through Christ who strengthens me" (Philippians 4:13). When I worry about my kids, my Dad reminds me, as he did when he gave me away when I got married, "Train up a child in the way he should go, and when he is old he will not depart from it" (Proverbs 22:6). When I get myself in a tizzy, my sister reminds me of God's assurance, "Don't be afraid, for I have ransomed you; I have called you by name; you are mine...when you go through deep waters and great trouble I will be with you -in rivers of difficulty, you will not drown" (Isaiah 43:1-3). I remind myself of the words in Isaiah 40:31 "They that wait upon the Lord shall renew their strength. They shall mount up with wings like eagles; they shall run and not be weary; they shall walk and not faint." It's not uncommon for us to call on each other for a little pick me up from time to time and when we do, you can best believe that the advice given is founded upon God's word. Amen.

You know, sometimes I just look around our big old dinner table and I cannot help but say "Thank you, Lord" for this gathering, for these incredibly beautiful, smart, and precious people I get to call "family." Just about the time I'm trying to get teary eyed and come into a little self-inflicted spell, I hear somebody hollerin' from the kitchen "Who wants dessert?" "Who's on clean up duty this week?" "Who wants a to-go plate?"

Lordhavemercy – It's Sunday Lunch and it's the best day of the week! Can I get a witness?

AUTHOR DISCLAIMER

Before anybody goes talking about the misprints in the recipes, a misplaced modifier in the narrative, whatever error you might feel compelled to bring to our attention, let us just say – we have been our own authors, editors, publishing company...you get the drift? It's entirely possible something won't be just exactly right. If you find that imperfection and you want to make that notation in your personal copy of the book, feel free and accept our apologies in advance. While the previous menus and the following recipes don't come near to summing up ALL that we have, we have chosen our most memorable to share with you. We're sure it's inevitable that one of us will eventually say, "Oh, why didn't we include this or that?" to which I can simply reply –you never know when a sequel might be coming!

APPETIZERS & BEVERAGES

Almond Tea

3 qt. water, divided
1 ½ c. sugar
1 tsp. vanilla

3 family-size tea bags
½ c. lemon juice
½ - 1 tsp. almond extract

Boil water and steep tea bags for 5 min. Add sugar and remaining ingredients.

Banana Crush Punch- Mom

4 c. sugar
6 c. water
2 ½ c. orange juice
½ c. lemon juice

4. c. pineapple juice
5 bananas (mashed)
1 (64 oz.) bottle lemon-lime carbonated beverage

Combine sugar and water in medium sauce pan. Cook over medium heat until sugar dissolves, stirring constantly. Add juices and bananas, mixing well. Pour into plastic container, cover and freeze. To serve, thaw slightly. Place in punch bowl and stir with fork to break into chunks. Add carbonated beverage.
Makes 5 ½ qts. (22 – 8 oz. cups or 35 punch cups)

Black Bean and Corn Salsa

1 can black-eyed peas
2 cans black beans
1 can golden corn
2 med. Tomatoes
1 chopped red pepper

1/3 c. cilantro
¼ c. lime juice (2 limes)
1 tsp. salt
1 T. olive oil
1 jalapeno

Combine and serve with tortilla chips.

Buffalo Chicken Dip

(Half this recipe for a small group)
2 cans of shredded chicken
(or 4 cooked chicken breasts)
12 oz. bottle of Texas Pete
hot sauce
2 (8 oz.) pkg. of cream
cheese
16 oz. bottle of ranch
dressing
8 oz. shredded cheddar
cheese
2 bags of Tostitos

Preheat oven to 350°. Shred chicken in bottom of a 13X9 dish. Pour hot sauce over chicken and mix together. In a saucepan, over medium heat, combine cream cheese and ranch dressing, stirring until smooth. Pour the mixture evenly over chicken and cook uncovered for 20 minutes. Sprinkle cheese over the top and bake uncovered for 10 minutes. Let stand 10 minutes before serving.

Flavor Craver Shrimp Dip

1//2 c. chili sauce
1 (8 oz.) pkg. cream cheese,
softened
½ c. mayonnaise
¼ c. chopped onion
2 tsp. horseradish sauce
1 (4½ oz.) can shrimp (or 1
frozen pkg. thawed)

Blend chili sauce into cream cheese. Mix in mayonnaise, onion, and horseradish. Fold in shrimp; chill. Serve with chips.

Fruit Dip

1 jar marshmallow crème
8 oz. cream cheese, softened
1 T. powdered sugar
1 tsp. lemon juice

Mix and serve with sliced apples, pineapple, melons and other fruit of choice.

Fruit Tea

4 c. boiled water
2 family tea bags
1 c. sugar
1 c. frozen lemonade
1 c. frozen orange juice
2 small cans apricot nectar
3 qt. ginger ale

Steep tea bags in boiling water for 5 minutes. Add remaining ingredients and chill.

LeConte Sunrise
(Serves 12)
4 C. orange juice
4 C. apple juice
6 Bananas

Blend all ingredients in a food processor. NOTE: It may require two batches. Place in freezer until almost frozen Re-blend and serve.

Party Punch (for 25 people)
1 pkg. lime Kool Aid to make 1 quart and add 2 cups sugar
1 c. pineapple juice
1 c. Lemon juice or 6-8 lemons
1 pt. orange juice or 8-10 oranges
1 large can grapefruit juice
2 bottles or more ginger ale

Heat just enough to dissolve sugar. Cool and then mix all ingredients except ginger ale which is added later. Before serving, add slices of oranges, lemons, and cherries.

Pizza Dip
1 (8 oz.) package cream cheese, softened
1 (14 oz.) jar of pizza sauce
1 ½ cups mozzarella cheese, shredded
Whatever topping you choose
(We use cooked ground beef and pepperonis. You can add onions, olives, sausage, etc.)
Corn Chips
Preheat oven to 350°. Press cream cheese in bottom of a 9" glass pie plate. Spread pizza sauce over cream cheese and layer remaining ingredients. Bake at 350° for 25 minutes. Serve with corn chips.

Russian Tea

½ c. instant tea
2. c. orange flavored drink
(Tang)
½ c. sweet lemonade mix

1 tsp. ground cloves
1 tsp. cinnamon
2 c. sugar

Mix all ingredients. Pour 3 tsp. in cup of very hot water. Stir.

Sausage Balls

1 lb. sausage
2 c. grated cheese

3 c. Bisquick
Paprika

Mix together and make into balls. Bake at 375°.

Sweet 'n Sour Meatballs

2 bottles chili sauce
1 c. grape jelly

4 tsp. lemon juice

Mix and put in large sauce pan or crockpot.
2 lb. ground beef
¼ c. minced onions

1 finely chopped bell pepper
1 stalk celery, finely chopped

Mix and shape into small balls. Cook in 2 T. oil and drain.
Simmer meat balls in sauce for 45 minutes in saucepan or on low heat in crockpot.

Sweet Tea

Bring 2 cups water to a boil in a saucepan. Remove pan from stove top. Steep 3 large family tea bags in hot water. Remove bags and pour water into 1 gallon pitcher. Add 1 ½ cups sugar and water to make 1 gallon.

Ambrosia
1 cup fruit cocktail
½ c. mandarin oranges
½ c. pineapple tidbits
½ c. mini marshmallows

¾ c. sour cream
¼ c. maraschino cherries
¼ c. red grapes

Mix and serve in a glass bowl.

Blueberry Salad
1 large pkg. grape Jell-O
1 c. boiling water
1 ½ c. fresh, frozen
(thawed), or canned
blueberries, drained
1 (8¼ oz.) can crushed
pineapple, drained (reserve
liquid)

1 (8 oz.) pkg. cream cheese,
softened
½ c. sugar
1 c. sour cream
½ tsp. vanilla
1 c. chopped pecans, divided
into two ½ cups

Dissolve Jell-O in boiling water. Add enough liquid form pineapple and enough water to make an additional cup of liquid. Stir in blueberries, pineapple, and ½ cup nuts. Pour into 2 quart flat dish; cover and chill until firm. Combine cream cheese, sugar, sour cream, and vanilla; spread over congealed salad. Sprinkle with ½ cup pecans.

Cherry Congealed Salad
1 lg. pkg. cherry Jell-O
1 c. boiling water
pineapple -drained
1 can cherry pie filling

¾ c. walnuts or pecans
1 (16-oz) can crushed

Mix first four ingredients. Add the crushed pineapple and refrigerate to congeal.

Cranberry Relish

Mix:
1 small box red Jell-O
1 c. boiling water

Stir until Jell-O is completely dissolved. Set aside.
In chopper or food processor, grind the following:
1 pkg. fresh whole cranberries
3 apples w/peel (remove core and seeds)
1 orange, including peel (remove seeds and end stems)
Mix:
1 c. crushed pineapple
2 cups sugar
1 cup chopped nuts (walnuts or pecans)

Mix all ingredients and chill. May be frozen for another meal.

Cranberry Salad

1 large pkg. cranberry Jell-O
1 ½ c. boiling water
1 (3 oz.) pkg. cream cheese
1 small can crushed
pineapple, drained
1 can whole cranberry sauce
½ c. chopped pecans

Dissolve Jell-O in water; set aside to cool. Mix cream cheese with small amount of pineapple juice. When well mixed, add pineapple, cranberry sauce, and nuts. Add to Jell-O mixture, chill.

Frozen Fruit Slush

2 c. boiling water
1 c. sugar - dissolve in water
1 (6 oz.) frozen orange juice
1 (8 oz.) crushed pineapple
1 (10 oz.) cherries with juice
4 sliced bananas
Mix and freeze. Allow to thaw before serving. Serve slushy. Serves 8-10.

Honey Walnut Fruit Salad

1/3 c. honey
½ c. light mayonnaise
½ c. chopped walnuts
3 cored, unpeeled red or
yellow apples, chopped
2 bananas, peeled and sliced

11 oz. can Mandarin oranges, drained

1 c. seedless grapes
1 T. lemon juice

Blend honey and mayonnaise until smooth. Toss remaining ingredients with lemon juice. Stir in honey mixture and refrigerate until ready to serve. Makes about 7 cups.

Mom's Frozen Fruit Salad

1 8oz. bar cream cheese
¾ c. sugar
1 (16 oz.) can crushed pineapple (use juice)
1 large pkg. frozen strawberries (use juice)
½ c. chopped pecans
1 large carton frozen whipped topping

Blend cream cheese and sugar. Add fruit and nuts. Fold in the cool whip. Place in large rectangular dish and freeze. If your dish is not larger than 9X13, you will need to use 2 smaller dishes. Cut in squares. Note: These can also be frozen in paper lined muffin tins.

Oriental Slaw

1 pkg. Ramen noodles (uncooked)
16 oz. slaw mix
½ sunflower seeds
½ c. slivered almonds
Dressing:

1/3 c. canola oil
½ tsp. salt
2 T. vinegar
1 pkg. seasoning from noodles
½ tsp. pepper

Mix all except noodles. Add noodles just before serving.

Orzo Pasta Salad
Boil 1 quart chicken stock
Add 1 c. orzo and cook approx. 15 minutes. Cool
Boil 2 ½ cups water and add 1 cup wheat berries.
Cool and add to orzo.
Add 1 can drained and rinsed garbanzo beans.
Add:
½ red onion finely diced (I often omit this.)
1 carton small baby tomatoes – halved
2 T. fresh chopped basil
1 T. fresh mint when in season
4 stalks celery sliced
Almonds, walnuts, or pecans to taste (any of these ingredients
can be added to or deleted!)
You can eat this with the dressing below or serve over a bed of
mixed greens and then add the dressing.
Dressing:
1 c. canola oil   Dash of garlic powder
½ c. balsamic vinegar OR   Couple dashes Heinz 57
red wine vinegar   steak sauce
½ c. sugar
(This can be refrigerated.)

Slaw
1 small cabbage head, finely   3 T. sugar
shredded   2 T. vinegar
½ large carrot, shredded   Salt and pepper to taste
½ c. mayonnaise   Celery seed to taste

Mix all ingredients and chill.

Strawberry Pretzel Salad
2 c. crushed pretzels
¾ c. melted butter
1 T. sugar
Mix together and press flat using a 9x13 inch pan. Bake at 400°
for 6 minutes. Cool well.

8 oz. cream cheese
1 c. sugar
9 oz. frozen whipped topping
Cream the cheese and beat in sugar. Fold in whipped topping. Put on top of pretzel crust.
Mix together:
6 oz. strawberry Jell-O
2 c. boiling water
1 (10 oz.) pkgs. frozen strawberries (use all juice)
Refrigerate for approximately 1 hour until it starts to gel. Add to other layers. Refrigerate until ready to eat.

Strawberry Salad
1 package ramen noodles, crushed, flavor packet discarded
1/4 c. sliced almonds
1/4 c. sunflower seeds
1/4 c. (1/2 stick) butter, melted
1 head romaine lettuce, washed and dried
One 5-ounce bag baby spinach
1 pint strawberries, hulled and thinly sliced
1 c. grated Parmesan
Dressing:

3/4 c. sugar	1/2 tsp. paprika
1/2 c. red wine vinegar	1/2 tsp. salt
3/4 c. vegetable oil	2 cloves garlic, minced

For the salad: Preheat the oven to 400 degrees F. In a small bowl, mix the ramen noodles, almonds, sunflower seeds and melted butter. Transfer to a baking sheet and toast in the oven, stirring occasionally, until browned, about 10 minutes. Remove from the oven and set aside to cool.
Tear the lettuce and combine with the spinach, strawberries and cheese in a large salad bowl.
For the dressing: Dissolve the sugar in the vinegar. Combine the oil, paprika, salt and garlic and then add to the sugar-vinegar mixture. Mix well and store in the refrigerator until ready to serve. Just before serving, sprinkle the crunchy topping over the salad green and toss the salad with enough dressing to coat the greens.

Aunt Betty's Texas Potatoes – Betty Lee

Melt 1 stick of margarine in 11X13 dish in 350° oven.
Mix:
2 cans cream of chicken soup
1 c. sour cream
Add: 1 large bag of thawed hash browns into the melted butter.
Mix the soup and sour cream mixture into the hash browns.
Add 2 sleeves Ritz crackers, crushed and ¾ stick melted
margarine.
Spread on top.
Bake 50-60 minutes on 350°.

Aunt Fanny's Baked Squash

(Aunt Fanny's was one of our favorite Atlanta restaurants.)

3 lbs. yellow squash	1 stick butter
1/2 c. chopped onions	1 T. sugar
½ c. cracker crumbs,	1 tsp. salt
½ tsp. pepper	1 c. shredded cheddar
2 eggs	cheese

Wash and cut up squash. Boil until tender, drain thoroughly, then
mash. Add all ingredients except ½ of butter to the squash. Melt
remaining butter. Pour mixture into baking dish then spread
melted butter over top and sprinkle with cracker crumbs and then
cheese. Bake 375° for approximately 1 hour or until brown on top.

Apricot Casserole

2 cans (15 ounces each) apricot halves
1/2 c. plus 2 T. butter, divided
1 c. packed brown sugar
1/4 c. all-purpose flour
1-1/3 c. crushed butter-flavored crackers (about 36 crackers)

Drain apricots, reserving 3/4 cup juice. Place apricots in a greased
11-in. x 7-in. baking dish. Melt 1/2 cup butter; add the brown
sugar, flour and reserved juice. Pour over apricots. Bake,

uncovered, at 350° for 20 minutes. Melt remaining butter; toss with crackers crumbs. Sprinkle over top. Bake 15-20 minutes longer or until golden brown.

Baked Asparagus

1 lb. asparagus
2 T. olive oil
Salt and black pepper to taste
1/2 cup loosely packed grated parmesan cheese, or to taste

Preheat oven to 400°. Break or cut off the woody ends of the asparagus spears. Arrange the asparagus spears on a foil-lined baking sheet and coat with the olive oil. Sprinkle with salt, pepper and the parmesan. Bake until the cheese begins to brown, about 8-10 minutes.

Baked Beans – Lori

2 large cans (28 oz.) pork and beans
½ c. Sweet Baby Rays Honey Barbeque Sauce
2 T. minced onion
2 T. yellow mustard
½ C. brown sugar
2 T. white Karo syrup
¼ C. white sugar
Sprinkle of cinnamon
½ C. ketchup
2 strips of bacon

Preheat oven to 350°. Mix all ingredients together in a 9X13 dish. Sprinkle just a dash of cinnamon on top of the beans. Place 2 strips of bacon side by side on top. Bake for 1 hour.

Beets

Feel free to prepare homemade beets if you choose. We're quite happy with beets from a jar found at your local grocery store. We like Aunt Nellie's brand.

Black-eyed Peas

1 lb. dried black-eyed peas
1 leftover ham bone or ham
hock
1 large onion, chopped

1 T. chopped garlic
1 stalk celery, chopped
8 c. of water
Salt and pepper to taste

Check black-eyed peas for pebble or discolored peas and discard. Rinse off peas. Add them and the ham bone or ham hock to a large pot with 8 cups of water. Add onion and celery. Season with salt and pepper. Bring the pot of peas to a boil, and then reduce heat to a low simmer. Cover pot and cook about 2 hours. Check and stir about every half hour. Add water if needed.

Broccoli Casserole

2 (10 oz.) pkg. frozen
chopped broccoli
1 can cream of mushroom
soup
1 T. grated onion
1 c. mayonnaise

1 c. grated sharp cheddar
cheese
2 beaten eggs
1 c. Ritz or cheese cracker
crumbs (usually one sleeve
of crackers works)
½ stick butter, melted

Cook broccoli according to directions on package. Drain well. Combine all ingredients except cracker crumbs and butter. Mix with broccoli. Combine cracker crumbs and melted butter and sprinkle on top of broccoli mixture. Bake at 400° for 25 minutes.

Brown Sugar Brussels Sprouts - Joan

1 lb. Brussels sprouts, halved
1 T. extra virgin olive oil
4 cloves garlic, crushed and
chopped
½ lemon, juiced

1 tsp. red pepper flakes
2 tsp. salt
2 T. balsamic vinegar
2 T. brown sugar

Steam Brussels sprouts over boiling water until tender, about 10-15 minutes. Heat oil and garlic over medium-high heat until fragrant, being careful not to burn. Add Brussels sprouts, lemon juice, pepper flakes and salt, stirring until they begin to brown, about 5 minutes. Add balsamic vinegar and brown sugar, stir for a minute and remove from heat, serve immediately.

Candied Sweet Potatoes

7 medium sweet potatoes pulp
1/4 c. butter 1/2 c. brown sugar
3/4 c. orange juice without 1/4 tsp. salt

Preheat oven to 400° and grease 13X9 baking dish. Boil sweet potatoes with skins on until tender. Drain. Let potatoes cool and then remove skins. Slice potatoes and layer in the baking dish. Combine butter, orange juice, brown sugar, and salt in a small saucepan until the butter melts and the sugar dissolves. Pour over potatoes and bake for 15 minutes.

Carrot Soufflé

5 c. carrots, cooked and mashed
1/2 c. butter, melted
3/4 c. sugar
2 T. flour

1 1/4 tsp. baking powder
2 eggs, beaten
1 T. vanilla extract
1/2 tsp. cinnamon

Blend all ingredients together. Pour carrot mixture into a greased casserole dish. Bake at 375° for 1 hour.

Collard Greens

1 chopped onion
1/2 tsp. minced garlic
3/4 pound smoked ham, chopped
3 (32-oz.) containers chicken broth

3 (1-lb.) packages fresh collard greens, washed and trimmed
1/3 c. apple cider vinegar
1 T. sugar
1 tsp. salt
3/4 tsp. pepper

Sauté onion in 1 T. olive oil. Add ham and garlic, and sauté 1 minute. Stir in broth and remaining ingredients. Cook 2 hours or to desired degree of tenderness.

Cooked Cabbage

1 head of cabbage
2 T. butter
2 T. olive oil
½ tsp. salt

½ tsp. of seasoning salt (or season to taste)
Black pepper
1½- 2 c. chicken broth (can also use water)

Cut cabbage into quarters, removing the hard stem. Slice each quarter into 1-inch wide strips. In a large pot, add butter, olive oil, salt, pepper, and cabbage. Add chicken broth and stir. Bring to a boil over medium-high heat. Cover and reduce heat to medium low. Simmer for 12-15 minutes, stirring occasionally until cabbage is tender. Do not overcook.

Cornbread Dressing

Large skillet of corn bread – crumbled
6 biscuits – crumbled
1 tsp. salt and pepper
4 T. sage
1 tsp. of poultry seasoning

5 cups broth
4 eggs, beaten
½ stick butter
1 c. minced onions
1 c. minced celery

Preheat oven to 350°. Butter a 9 x 13 inch pan and set aside. Melt butter in a skillet over medium heat. Sauté the onion and celery; add the salt, pepper, sage and poultry seasoning. Continue cooking and stirring for 2 minutes. Set aside to cool. Combine the crumbled cornbread and bread into a large bowl. Add sautéed veggies; add 4 cups of broth. Taste and adjust seasonings. Add the beaten eggs; gently toss. Add more of the broth as needed, taking care not to make the dressing too soupy. Dressing should be the consistency of cooked oatmeal. Lightly spoon into the casserole dish, but do not pack down. Bake at 350° for 45 minutes. For a moister stuffing, baked covered. For a drier stuffing with a crunchy top, bake uncovered.

For Sausage Dressing: Brown and drain a 1 pound roll of pork sausage. Set aside and stir into the dressing just before it goes into the oven.

Corn Casserole

Melt 1 stick butter.
Add:

1 can cream style corn
1 can whole kernel corn
(juice and all)

1 c. sour cream
1 pkg. Jiffy corn bread muffin mix

Mix. Pour into 2 quart casserole or 9x13 inch pan. Bake at 350° for 1 hour.

Corn on the Cob

Shuck and clean 6 ears of corn. Mix ½ c. mayonnaise, 1 c. shredded parmesan cheese, 1 tsp. salt, and 1 tsp. pepper. Spread over each corn cob. Wrap corn in aluminum foil and grill 10 minutes. May use additional sauce to spread on cooked corn.

Crash Hot Potatoes - Cathy

12 whole New Potatoes (or Other Small Round Potatoes)

3 T. olive oil
Kosher salt to taste

Black pepper to taste
Rosemary

Bring a pot of salted water to a boil. Add in as many potatoes as you wish to make and cook them until they are fork-tender.

On a sheet pan, generously drizzle olive oil. Place tender potatoes on the cookie sheet leaving plenty of room between each potato. With a potato masher, gently press down each potato until it slightly mashes, rotate the potato masher 90 degrees and mash again. Brush the tops of each crushed potato generously with more olive oil.

Sprinkle potatoes with kosher salt, fresh ground black pepper and fresh chopped rosemary (or chives or thyme or whatever herb you have available.)

Bake in a 450° oven for 20-25 minutes until golden brown.

Crock Pot Macaroni & Cheese - Lori

(This recipe makes enough for the entire Sunday Lunch gang. Cut recipe in half if cooking for a smaller group.)

16 oz. box of cooked macaroni
2 T. butter
3 12.oz. cans evaporated milk

6 c. Cheddar cheese, shredded
2 tsp. salt
½ tsp. black pepper

Cook macaroni per directions on the box, drain, and pour into the crock pot dish. Cut up the butter and let melt on the hot macaroni. Stir in evaporated milk, cheese, salt and pepper. After stirring all ingredients together, cover and cook on medium 2 to 3 hours.

Curried Fruit

1 (16 oz.) can sliced pears, well drained
1 (20 oz.) can pineapple chunks, drained
1 (15 oz.) can apricot halves, drained
2 (15 oz.) cans sliced peaches

1 (4 oz.) jar maraschino cherries (optional)
1/4 c. packed brown sugar
1/4 c. white sugar
3 tsp. curry powder
2 T. butter

Preheat oven to 400°. Drain the fruit and arrange it in an oven-proof casserole dish. Dot the fruit with butter or margarine. Mix the sugars and the curry powder together, sprinkle over the top of the fruit. Bake until slightly brown, about 15 to 20 minutes.

Fried Okra

10 pods okra, sliced in ¼ in. pieces
1 egg, beaten
1 c. cornmeal

¼ tsp. salt
¼ tsp. ground black pepper
½ c. canola oil

In a small bowl, soak okra in egg for 5 to 10 minutes. In a medium bowl, combine cornmeal, salt, and pepper.
Heat oil in a large skillet over medium-high heat. Dredge okra in the cornmeal mixture, coating evenly. Carefully place okra in hot oil; stir continuously. Reduce heat to medium when okra first starts to brown, and cook until golden. Drain on paper towels.

Deviled Eggs - Lori

6 eggs, hard boiled
¼ c. mayonnaise
Paprika
1/8 tsp. pepper
1/8 tsp. salt

1 tsp. yellow mustard
1 T. sweet pickle relish

Dash of onion powder

Slice the eggs in half and spoon out the yolks and put into a bowl. Place the whites on a serving dish and put aside. Mash the yolks with a fork and add all the other ingredients to the bowl except the paprika. Mix until smooth. Spoon the mixture into the egg whites and gently run a fork over the filling to add a texture to the yolk mix. Top with Paprika. Refrigerate until ready to serve.

Glazed Carrots - Cathy

1 lb. carrots, cut into 1-in. pieces
1 c. water
¼ tsp. salt
½ c. orange juice

1 tsp. grated orange rind
2 tsp. cornstarch
2 T. butter
2 T. honey

Cook carrot pieces in 1 cup boiling water with salt in a medium saucepan 10 minutes or until tender, drain carrot, and place in a serving bowl. Stir together orange juice and cornstarch in a small saucepan until smooth. Stir in butter and honey; cook over medium heat, stirring constantly, 4 minutes or until thickened. Pour over carrot, and toss to coat.

Green Beans – Fresh

(We don't do canned green beans. We know some of you try to fancy them up, but we can always tell, always. ☺)

2 lbs. fresh green beans   5 oz. salt pork
4 ½ c. water

Rinse, trim, and snap green beans in half or thirds. Place into a large saucepan with water and salt pork. Bring to a boil. Reduce to a very low simmer, cover, and let barely simmer for 1 to 1 ½ hours or until desired tenderness.

Green Peas

Purchase our favorite brand of peas – LeSuer.

Green Bean Casserole – Josh

1 can (10 1/2 ounces) condensed cream of mushroom soup
1/2 c. milk   4 c. cooked cut green beans
1 tsp. soy sauce   1 1/3 c. canned French fried
1 dash black pepper

Stir the soup, milk, soy sauce, black pepper, beans and 2/3 cup onions in a 1 1/2-quart casserole. Bake at 350° for 25 minutes or until the bean mixture is hot and bubbling. Stir the bean mixture. Sprinkle with the remaining onions. Bake for 5 minutes or until the onions are golden brown.

Green Bean Casserole - Chase

(adapted from Alton Brown from The Food Network)
For the topping:
2 medium onions, thinly   2 T. panko bread crumbs
sliced   1 tsp. salt
¼ c. all-purpose flour

Nonstick cooking spray
For beans and sauce:
2 T. plus 1 tsp. salt, divided   2 T. butter
1 lb. fresh green beans,   12 oz. mushrooms, trimmed
rinsed, trimmed and halved   and cut into ½ inch pieces

101

½ tsp. freshly ground black pepper

2 cloves garlic, minced

¼ tsp. ground nutmeg

2 T. all-purpose flour

1 c. chicken broth

1 c. half-and-half

Preheat oven to 475°. Combine the onions, flour, panko and salt in a large mixing bowl and toss to combine. Coat a sheet pan with nonstick cooking spray and evenly spread the onions on the pan. Place the pan on the middle rack of the oven and bake until golden brown, approximately 30 minutes. Toss the onions 2 to 3 times during cooking. Once done, remove from the oven and set aside until ready to use. Turn the oven down to 400°. While the onions are cooking, prepare the beans. Bring a gallon of water and 2 Tbsp. of salt to a boil in an 8-quart saucepan. Add the beans and blanch for 5 minutes. Drain in a colander and immediately plunge the beans in cold water to stop the cooking. Drain and set aside. Melt the butter in a 12-inch cast iron skillet set over medium-high heat. Add the mushrooms, 1 teaspoon salt and pepper and cook, stirring occasionally, until the mushrooms begin to give up some of their liquid, approximately 4 to 5 minutes. Add the garlic and nutmeg and continue to cook for another 1 to 2 minutes. Sprinkle the flour over the mixture and stir to combine. Cook for 1 minute. Add the broth and simmer for 1 minute. Decrease the heat to medium-low and add the half-and-half. Cook until the mixture thickens, stirring occasionally, approximately 6 to 8 minutes.

Remove the heat and stir in ¼ of the onions and all of the green beans. Top with the remaining onions. Place into the oven and bake until bubbly, approximately 15 minutes. Remove and serve immediately.

Mashed Potatoes

(We make a large bowl of potatoes for our crowd. This will feed about 15.)

5 lbs. Yukon gold potatoes, peeled and cut into 2-inch pieces
½ c. whipping cream

½ c. milk
½ c. butter, melted
2 ½ tsp. salt
½ tsp. pepper

Bring potatoes and cold water to cover to a boil in a large Dutch oven. If desired, add 1 tsp. minced garlic. Boil 25 minutes or until tender. Drain. Place back in Dutch oven, and heat a few minutes over low heat until potatoes are dry. Heat whipping cream and milk in a small saucepan over low heat 4 minutes or just until warm. Remove from heat. Add milk, whipping cream, butter, salt, and pepper to potatoes. Use either a hand masher to mash the mixture or use a mixer. Serve immediately.

Mixed Vegetable Casserole

1 can mixed vegetables drained
1 c. mayonnaise
½ c. onion

1 c. grated cheddar cheese
1 sleeve Ritz crackers
2 T. butter

Mix all together. Crumble Ritz crackers on top and dot with butter. Bake 350° for 20 minutes.

Old-Fashioned Mac and Cheese

1 – 7oz package of macaroni noodles
3 T. butter
3 T. flour
2 ½ c. milk

½ tsp. salt
1/8 tsp. pepper
1/8 tsp. paprika
2 cc. grated cheese

Cook mac according to package directions. Blend butter and flour in saucepan. Add milk gradually. Cook on medium heat until creamy. Add noodles, salt, pepper, and paprika. Pour into well-greased 2 qt. casserole and sprinkle cheese on top. Bake at 375° for 30 minutes.

Pineapple Cheese Casserole

1 can pineapple tidbits, drained. Reserve 3 T juice.

1 c. cheddar cheese, grated   ¼ c. butter

½ c. sugar   ¾ sleeve Ritz crackers

3 T. plain flour

Mix pineapple and cheese. Mix sugar, pineapple juice and flour. Mix together and pour into buttered glass dish. Melt butter and mix with crushed Ritz crackers. Spread over pineapple mixture. Bake at 350° for 25 or 30 minutes.

Pinto Beans

1 lb. dry pinto beans   Approx. ¼ lb. salt pork

Rinse dried pintos under cool water and drain. Put them into a large bowl and cover with water to soak overnight. This helps cut down on cooking time and take some of the "gas" out. In the morning, rinse beans well with cool water, drain and then put in crock pot. Fill with water about an inch or 2 above beans. Cook on low all day for about 8-9 hours. Add salt, as needed.

We serve this with cornbread and our favorite Chow Chow from the Old Mill Restaurant in Pigeon, Forge, TN, one of our family getaway destinations.

Potato Salad Robbs

5 lb. bag red potatoes

Wash and cut them into chunks with the peel on (about 2 inches). Place in large pan and cover with water. Add ½ cup chopped onions and ½ tsp salt and bring to a boil. Reduce heat to medium and cook for approximately 20 minutes or until potatoes are fork tender. Drain and allow potatoes to cool for about 20 minutes. Chop 5 hard-boiled eggs and add to potatoes. Mash some of the potatoes and leave the rest in cubes according to your preference.

In a separate container mix the following:

¾ cups mayonnaise   ½ cup pickle relish

1 T. mustard   2 tsp. salt

1 T. apple cider vinegar   1 tsp. celery seed

1 jar pimentos (drained)

Add to potatoes and eggs and mix. Sprinkle with paprika and chill.

Potato Wedges

6 med. potatoes
½ tsp. salt
Dash cayenne pepper
Dash pepper

1 tsp. dried rosemary
2 T. olive oil
1/3 c. Parmesan cheese

Scrub unpeeled potatoes. Cut potatoes into wedges, lengthwise. Cover with water and dash salt. Boil wedges for 5 minutes, drain, and pat dry. Spread wedges in single layer on lightly greased baking sheet. Sprinkle with oil, spices, and herbs. Bake at 425° for 15 minutes. Sprinkle with cheese.

Rice Casserole

1 c. long-grain rice
1 stick butter, melted
1 can beef consommé soup

1 can onion soup
1 small can sliced
mushrooms

Mix all ingredients in a 1 ½ quart casserole dish and bake uncovered at 325° for 1 hour.

Roasted Fall Veggies - Lori

1 medium butternut squash, peeled, seeded, and cut into squares
10 red new potatoes, cleaned and cut into quarters
3 large zucchini, cleaned, and cut into squares
3 large yellow squash, cleaned, and cut into squares
3 sweet potatoes, peeled, cut into squares
½ pkg. baby carrots
1 red onion, peeled, quartered
1 pkg. dry Italian dressing mix
3T olive oil

Preheat oven to 400°. Line baking pan with parchment paper. Toss cut up vegetables with olive oil and spread onto the cookie sheet baking pan. Sprinkle with package of Italian dressing mix. Salt and pepper, if desired. Bake on 400 for 30 minutes.

Roasted, Smashed, and Loaded Potatoes- Cathy
1 lb. small red bliss potatoes
6 T. garlic-infused olive oil, divided
Kosher salt and freshly cracked black pepper
1/2 c. finely grated Parmigiano-Reggiano
1/2 c. sour cream
Potato toppings as desired (bacon, chives, scallions, cheese)

Preheat the oven to 450°. Adjust the oven racks to the top and bottom positions. Place the potatoes on a sheet pan, pour 3/4 cup water over the potatoes and cover tightly with foil. Bake on the bottom rack until tender, about 30 minutes. Remove from the oven, drain any remaining water and let rest 8 minutes. Drizzle 3 tablespoons oil over the potatoes, making sure they are evenly coasted. Space the potatoes evenly on the sheet pan and, using a potato masher, flatten the potatoes to about 1/2 inch thick (about 1/2 the length of your thumb to the first joint). Sprinkle with salt and pepper. Drizzle the remaining 3 tablespoons olive oil over the potatoes and roast on the top rack for 15 minutes. Remove from the oven and sprinkle with the cheese. Roast on the bottom rack until golden brown, about 20 minutes. Remove from the oven and top with the sour cream and other toppings. Serve immediately.

Roasted Vegetables
Select seasonal vegetables such as red potatoes, squash, red onions, carrots.
Preheat oven to 450°. Place vegetables on rimmed baking sheets (line with parchment paper for easy cleanup).
Toss with olive oil, salt, and pepper to taste. Roast until vegetables are tender and beginning to brown, about 30-45 minutes. Serve hot or at room temperature.

Scalloped Tomatoes

¼ c. minced onions
3 T. butter
2 c. soft bread crumbs
½ tsp. sugar
1 tsp. salt

¼ tsp. pepper
Dash cayenne pepper
3 ½ c. tomatoes
¼ c. soft bread crumbs
1 T. melted butter

Sauté onions in 3 T. butter. Add next 5 ingredients. Arrange a layer of tomatoes in the bottom of a greased 1 ½ qt. casserole dish. Top with a layer of onion and bread mixture. Continue to layer. Combine ¼ cup soft bread crumbs and I T. butter. Sprinkle on top of casserole. Bake at 375° for 45 minutes.

Shaker Corn Pudding- Cathy

2 c. corn, frozen or fresh
2 T. flour
1 tsp. salt
3 T. butter

3 whole eggs
2 T. sugar
1 3/4 c. milk

Blend butter, sugar, flour and salt. Add eggs, beating well. Stir in corn and milk. Pour ingredients into buttered casserole and bake. Stir half-way through baking time with oven temperature at 325° for 45 minutes. Test by a silver knife inserted comes out clean. Pudding will be golden brown. Frozen corn or fresh corn can be chopped or kernels left whole. Mixture can be made ahead of baking and kept in jar in refrigerator. Shake well and pour into baking dish.

Spring Potato Toss

Gently toss together cooked quartered small red potatoes with green peas, refrigerated pesto, and lemon juice. Sprinkle with cooked, crumbled bacon.

Squash Casserole

Cook and drain 3 lbs. squash. Add:
1/2 stick butter
½ c. chopped onions

½ c. cracker crumbs
½ tsp. black pepper

1 tsp. salt   2 eggs
1 T. butter
Place in butter baking dish. Sprinkle top with butter bread crumbs.
Bake 375° for 1 hour.

Squash Dressing
Cook 8 squash with ½ c. chopped onion.
Drain and add 1 stick butter.
Combine the following:

2 eggs   1 can cream of chicken soup
2 c. of corn bread or   1 tsp. salt
Pepperidge Farm dressing   ¼ tsp. pepper
mix   1 T. sage

Add mixture to squash and pour in greased 2 quart casserole dish.
Cook at 400° for 30 minutes or until bubbly.

Sweet Potato Casserole - Lori
3 c. mashed sweet potatoes (About 6 med. Sweet potatoes)
1 c. sugar   1/3 c. butter
½ tsp. salt   ½ c. milk
2 eggs   1 tsp. vanilla
Mix all together and pour into dish.

Topping
1 c. brown sugar   ½ c. flour
1 c. chopped pecans   1/3 stick melted butter
Stir and pour on the potatoes.
Bake at 350° for 35 minutes

Town and Country Candied Sweet Potatoes
6 sweet potatoes   2 tsp. cinnamon
¼ pound butter   ½ tsp. nutmeg
1 c. sugar   1 tsp. vanilla extract

Steam sweet potatoes 20 minutes. Let cool before cutting. Cut
sweet potatoes in quarters. Place in pan and add all ingredients.
Bake at 400° for 30 minutes.

Twice Baked Potatoes

6 medium to large baking potatoes
Rub each potato skin with butter and salt them.
Bake at 425° for 1 hour. Let potatoes cool in order to better handle them.

1/3 c. 2% milk	Salt
6 T. butter	Pepper
1 c. sharp shredded cheese	Bacon pieces (optional)
¼ c. sour cream	

Scoop out the insides of the potato with a spoon. Mash the potatoes in a bowl and add milk, butter, sour cream, salt and pepper. After they are mashed, spoon them back into the potato skins. Top each potato with cheese and other optional ingredients, if desired. Put back in the oven and bake on 350° for 10 minutes, just to melt the cheese.

White Beans

4 cups dried white beans, rinsed and drained
1 ham hock or ham bone, with some ham remaining
2 tsp. salt   Black or white pepper to
                                            taste

Place beans in a large pot. Fill water to four inches over the beans. Bring to a boil over medium high heat on top of stove. Add ham hock or bone, salt and pepper. Reduce and simmer covered for three hours or until beans are soft. Add water as needed to keep beans covered. We like them cooked extra soft!

MAIN DISHES

Apricot Chicken

6-8 boneless, skinless
chicken breasts
1 jar apricot preserves

1 pkg. onion soup mix
8 oz. Russian dressing

Place all ingredients in a slow cooker. Cook for 4-5 hours on low
or 3-4 hours on high.

Baked London Broil

2 ½ lbs. London broil (flat cut)
1 (10 oz.) bottle steak sauce
2 T. lemon juice
2-3 lg. onions, peeled and thinly sliced and separated
2-3 tsp. minced garlic

In a large 9 x 13 inch casserole dish, spread a bed of the
separated onion slices (about 1/3 or enough to cover the bottom
of the dish) and drizzle with the mixture of steak sauce and lemon
juice (about ¼ of the mixture). Wash and pat dry meat. Salt to
taste and rub remaining garlic on top side and cover with the rest
of the onion rings. Drizzle remaining sauce mixture over meat.
Cover tightly with plastic wrap and marinate overnight. Remove
plastic wrap and cover tightly with aluminum foil and place in
preheated 350° oven for approximately 3 hours. Check with fork
for tenderness. If not tender, recover and bake another 20-30
minutes. Slice cross grain and enjoy. Leftovers can be refrigerated
and reheated, covered, at 350° for 30 minutes.

Baked Shrimp

Melt a stick of butter in the pan covered with aluminum foil. Slice
one lemon and layer it on top of the butter. Put down 3 dozen
fresh shrimp, then sprinkle one pack of dried Italian seasoning.
Put in the oven and bake at 350 for 15 min.

Baked Spaghetti (Paula Dean)

8 ounces uncooked angel hair pasta
1/4 c. chopped fresh parsley
1 1/2 lbs. ground beef
1 1/2 tsp. Paula Deen's House Seasoning
1 1/2 tsp. sugar
1 1/2 tsp. seasoning salt
1 1/2 tsp. Italian seasoning
2 c. tomato sauce
1 c. water
2 c. canned diced tomatoes
2 cloves garlic, chopped
1/2 c. diced green bell pepper
1/2 c. diced onion
1 c. grated cheddar cheese
1 c. Monterey Jack cheese
2 small bay leaves

Preheat oven to 350°. In a stockpot, combine the tomatoes, tomato sauce, water, onions, peppers, garlic, parsley, seasoning mixtures, sugar, and bay leaves. Bring to a boil over high heat, and then reduce the heat and let simmer, covered, for 1 hour. Crumble the ground beef in a large skillet. Cook over medium-high heat until fully cooked, with no pink color remaining. Drain the fat from the meat, and then add the ground beef to the stockpot. Simmer for 20 more minutes. Cook the pasta according to the package directions. Cover the bottom of a 13 by 9 by 2-inch pan with sauce. Add a layer of pasta and then a little less than 1/2 of each cheese; repeat the layers, ending with the sauce. Bake in the oven for 30 minutes. Top the casserole with the remaining cheese, return it to the oven, and continue to cook until the cheese is melted and bubbly, about 5 more minutes. Cut into squares before serving.

Baked Beef Brisket- Joan

1 (6 lb.) brisket
2 pkg. onion soup mix
6 cloves garlic, crushed
1 ½ c. ketchup
1 ½ lbs. carrots, peeled and cut into sticks

Preheat oven to 350°. Place brisket in a large baking dish and sprinkle soup mix over meat. Cover with ketchup and 2 cups water; add crushed garlic. Cover with foil and bake for 2 ½ hours. Next place carrots on top of brisket and continue to bake for another hour. Refrigerate brisket and carrots overnight or up to 2 days to maximize flavor. One hour before serving: Preheat oven to 350°. Slice brisket against the grain into thin slices. Return sliced brisket to baking dish and top with carrots. Cover with foil and bake for an hour or until brisket is heated through.

Beef Stew - Mom

1 lb. stew meat
Boil in half pan of water and simmer 1 ½ hours. Add one quartered onion, 1 tsp. salt, and 4 sliced carrots. Cook 30 min. Add 1 (15 oz.) can tomato sauce, ½ tsp. celery seed, 4 peeled and sliced potatoes. Cook until tender. Make paste of 1 T. flour and ¼ c. water to thicken. Temper the paste with a small amount of stew and add to stew. Add salt and pepper to taste.

Breakfast Casserole - Joan

Brown 1 lb. bulk sausage. Add onions, green peppers, or mushrooms, as desired. Combine the following: 6 eggs, 2 c. milk, 6 slices bread (torn in pieces), 8 oz. cheese, shredded cheddar. Mix sausage with other ingredients. Pour into greased or sprayed 9x13" pan. Bake 350° for 45-60 minutes. 12 servings.

Cheese Strata

4 eggs
1 ¾ c. milk
1 sm. minced onion
1/8 tsp. paprika

1/8 tsp. red pepper
½ tsp. dry mustard
¼ tsp. black pepper
¼ tsp. Worcester sauce

Mix and set aside.
Trim crust of 6 slices of white bread and cut into 9 square pieces. Grate 2 c. med cheddar cheese. Spray 8 x 10 dish. Layer bread, cheese, bread, cheese. Pour liquid mixture on top. Cover and refrigerate overnight. Remove ½ hour before baking. Bake 300° 1 hour.

Chicken Fingers - Mom

Heat cooking oil in a deep skillet or deep fryer. Place enough flour in flat dish to coat each piece of chicken. Salt and pepper chicken pieces to taste. Coat each piece thoroughly with flour. Place chicken pieces in deep oil and turn frequently until brown. Do not overload cooking oil, but allow pieces to cook uniformly. Place pieces when done on paper towels so excess oil can drain off pieces.

Chicken and Wild Rice Casserole

Two 6-ounce boxes long-grain and wild rice mix, such as Uncle Ben's
1 c. (2 sticks) unsalted butter, plus more for greasing dish
16 ounces fresh mushrooms, sliced, or two 4 1/2-ounce cans sliced mushrooms, drained (reserve the liquid)
1 small onion, chopped
1/2 c. all-purpose flour
3 c. chicken broth
3 c. half-and-half
4 cooked boneless, skinless chicken breast halves, diced
1 c. toasted slivered almonds, coarsely chopped
1/2 c. sliced pimientos
1/4 c. chopped fresh parsley
1 tsp. kosher salt
1/2 tsp. freshly ground black pepper

Cook the long-grain and wild rice mixes according to the package directions. Set aside. Preheat the oven to 350°. Grease a 9-by-13-by-2-inch casserole dish. In a large skillet, melt the butter. Add the mushrooms and onions and sauté until the onions are translucent. Stir in the flour, cooking for 2 to 3 minutes. Slowly stir the broth (and reserved canned mushroom liquid if using) into the onion mixture, then stir in the half-and-half. Cook until the mixture has thickened, 7 to 10 minutes. Add the chicken, rice, toasted almonds, pimientos, parsley, salt and pepper into the wet mixture. Pour everything into the prepared casserole dish and bake, uncovered, until most of the liquid has been absorbed, 30 to 45 minutes.

Chicken Chili - Cathy

1 tsp. oil
1 lb. ground chicken
1T. bottled chopped garlic
2 cans (14 ½ oz each) diced tomatoes with jalapeno peppers
2 tsp. each ground cumin and chili powder, preferably Mexican style
1 can (15 ¼ oz.) kidney beans
1 can (15 oz.) black beans
1 can (15 ¼ oz.) whole kernel corn
Accompaniments: sour cream, shredded Mexican-style Cheddar-jack cheese and tortilla chips

Heat oil in a large nonstick skillet over medium-high heat. Add chicken and cook, breaking up chunks, 5 minutes or until browned. Add the garlic, tomatoes and spices. Cover and simmer 5 minutes, stirring occasionally. Stir in beans and corn, cover and heat through. Serve with sour cream, cheese and chips.

Chicken Cordon Bleu with Bleu Cheese Dressing

2. c. mayonnaise
6 T. buttermilk
4 oz. crumbled bleu cheese
1/s tsp. lemon juices
Dash of tobacco,
Worcestershire, pepper
Mix with whisk. Coat 12-15 chicken in dressing and refrigerate 2 hours. Sprinkle cooked bacon on top. Bake 40-50 minutes at 325°.

Chicken Divan

2 pkgs. frozen broccoli
2 cans cream of chicken soup
1 c. mayonnaise
½ tsp. curry powder
½ c. soft buttered bread cut into cubes

2 c. cooked chicken
1 tsp. lemon juice
½ c. sharp cheddar cheese
1 T. melted butter

Cook broccoli and drain. Put in buttered casserole dish. Put chicken on top. Combine soup, mayo, lemon, and curry and pour over chicken. Sprinkle with cheese. Combine bread cubes and melted butter and put on top. Bake on 350° for 25-30 minutes.

Chicken Enchiladas

8 c. chopped cooked chicken
1 (28 oz.) can tomatoes with green chiles, well drained
1 (15 oz.) can black beans, rinsed and drained
1 (10.75 oz.) can cream of chicken soup
3 c. shredded Monterey Jack cheese, divided
1 c. sour cream   1 tsp. chili powder
2 tsp. ground cumin   1 tsp. salt
2 tsp. garlic powder
8 medium soft taco flour tortillas
1 (10 oz.) can mild green chile enchilada sauce

Preheat oven to 350°. Spray a 13x9 inch baking dish with nonstick cooking spray. In a large bowl, combine chicken, tomatoes with chiles, black beans, soup, 2 cups cheese, sour cream, cumin, garlic powder, chili powder, and salt, stirring to combine well. Spoon 1 cup chicken mixture down center or each tortilla; roll up tortilla tightly. Place enchiladas, seam side down, in a single layer in prepared baking dish; top with enchilada sauce. Sprinkle evenly with remaining 1 cup cheese. Bake for 30 – 35 minutes or until hot and bubbly. Serve immediately. Serves 8

Chicken Pot Pie

½ stick butter, melted   1 can drained peas and
1/3 c. flour   carrots
2 c. chicken broth   ½ tsp. salt
1 c. milk   ¼ tsp. pepper
2 c. meat   ¼ tsp. celery seed

Combine butter, flour, broth, and milk in pan. Cook on medium heat, stirring till thick. Add chick, peas and carrots, and seasonings. Pour into 2 qt. buttered casserole and cover with pie crust. Bake at 425° for 25 minutes.

Chicken with Chipped Beef

1 (2 oz.) package chipped beef
6 skinless, boneless chicken breast halves
1 (10.75 oz.) can condensed cream of mushroom soup
1 (8 oz.) container sour cream
1/2 tsp. paprika
6 bacon strips

Preheat oven to 275°. Line the bottom of a 9x13 inch baking dish with slices of chipped beef. Place chicken breasts wrapped bacon on top of chipped beef. In a medium bowl, mix together condensed soup and sour cream. Pour sour cream mixture over chicken breasts, and sprinkle with paprika. Cover and bake in preheated oven for about 3 hours. Uncover the last 15 or 20 minutes to let the bacon brown. *Each breast can be fixed the day before and have them ready to spoon the soups over when ready to bake.
 Option: Replace chipped beef with a 12 oz. pkg. country ham.

Chili – Cathy's

5 cans pinto beans
2 T. oil
1 – 2 lbs. ground beef
1 lg. onion, chopped*
2-3 tsp. minced garlic
1 bay leaf
3 T. chili powder
1 T. paprika

1 T. oregano
1 T. ground cumin
1 large can crushed tomatoes
1 tsp. salt
½ tsp. pepper
¾ tsp. cayenne pepper or to taste

*(I sometimes use frozen chopped onions from the grocery freezer section)

In large pot heat oil and brown beef, onion and garlic. Drain grease. Combine the remaining ingredients in the pot. Simmer slowly for 2-3 hours, stirring occasionally. This can also be prepared in a large crockpot.

Chili – Chuck's

2 T. butter
Large onion, chopped
3 lb. ground beef
1 lb. mild sausage
3 cloves garlic
5 T. hot chili powder
4 T. mild chili powder
2 tsp. cumin

3 c. hot water with beef bouillon
1 T. oregano
1 ½ tsp. salt
1 (16 oz.) cans stewed tomatoes
4 (16 oz.) cans pinto beans

2 T. masa harina (corn meal), mixed with water to form paste

Cook onion in butter. Add beef, sausage, garlic, hot and mild chili powders, cumin, salt, and oregano. Cook until beef and sausage are brown. Add water and tomatoes, bring to a boil. Lower heat and simmer to 2½ to 3 hours, uncovered. Add beans and masa harina; simmer for 30 minutes.

Chili – Lori's

1 lb. ground beef
5 cans pinto beans
5 cans dark red kidney beans

1 can whole stewed tomatoes
6 T. chili powder
1 Bay leaf

In a 5qt Dutch oven, brown ground beef. Drain, clean excess grease from the pot and return the beef to the Dutch oven. Add the can of tomatoes, slicing each tomato into smaller pieces. Add each can of pinto and kidney beans and stir all together. Use 2 of the cans and fill with water to add to mixture. Add the Chili powder and adjust to your taste. Add bay leaf last and after bringing the mixture to a boil, turn down the heat to low, cover, and simmer for several hours. Remove bay leaf before serving.

Coca-Cola Ham

Large Butt Portion ham – de-boned. Line bottom of roasting pan with foil. Spray foil with Pam. Place ham on foil
Pour 1 can of Coke over ham and add water to fill pan with 2" liquid. Cook at 250° approx. 8 hours. When cooked, pull apart and place on platter. For topping –

Mix 1 c. brown sugar, ½ to 1 T. mustard and Coke until runny. Pour over ham. Cover with foil until served.

Corn Chowder

5 slices bacon, cooked and crumbled (save 3 T. grease)
1 med. Onion, cooked in grease until lightly browned
Add:

2 cans cream style yellow corn

1 can whole kernel corn

1 c. diced potatoes, cooked

1 can cream of mushroom soup

3 c. milk

1 tsp. salt

¼ tsp. white pepper

Bring to a boil, stirring well. Cover and simmer for 30 minutes.

Country Style Steak - Mom

Select cube steak pieces slightly smaller than an adult hand. Prepare an electric skillet with sufficient cooking oil to cover the bottom of the skillet. Place enough flour in a flat dish to coat both sides of the steak. Season steak pieces with salt and pepper to taste. Place each steak piece individually in flour and turn to coat both sides thoroughly. Place steak pieces in hot electric skillet. Brown each piece by turning frequently. After all pieces are brown, add sufficient water to skillet to barely cover steak. Continue turning until steak is well done. Place lid on skillet and turn heat to warm or low until ready to serve.

Cranberry Chicken

6-8 boneless, skinless chicken breasts

1 (16-20 oz.) can whole cranberry sauce

1 pkg. onion soup mix

8 oz. Russian dressing

Place all ingredients in a slow cooker. Cook for 4-5 hours on low or 3-4 hours on high.

Crock Pot Beef Bourguignon
(Cathy's crockpot version on Julia Child's recipe)

1 c. dry red wine
2 T. olive oil
1 large onion, sliced
½ tsp. thyme
2 T. parsley, chopped
1 bay leaf
¼ tsp pepper
2 pounds stewing beef, cut into 1 ½ inch cubes

3 slices bacon (thick cut), diced
1 T. flour
12 small white onions
1 carrot, sliced
½ pound sliced mushrooms
2 cloves garlic, minced
1 T. tomato paste
2 c. beef stock
1 tsp salt

Mix 1st seven ingredients and add beef. Marinate at least 3 hrs. or overnight. In skillet, sauté bacon and remove. Remove beef from marinade. Dry with a paper towel and then dust the beef with flour. Sauté beef until lightly browned. Brown the carrots, mushrooms, and white onions. Place all in crock pot. Add remaining ingredients: garlic, tomato paste, beef stock, and salt. Cook on low 8-10 hours. To thicken the stew, prepare a roux by melting 2 T. butter with the same quantity of flour. Add juice from stew to the roux and then pour the mix back into the stew.

Crock Pot Italian Chicken
6 boneless, skinless chicken breasts
Salt and pepper to taste
¼ teaspoon garlic powder
1 bottle Kraft Zesty Italian Salad Dressing

Place chicken breasts in bottom of crock pot. Sprinkle with salt, pepper, and garlic powder. Pour Italian dressing over chicken. Turn chicken over with tongs to make sure they are good and covered by the dressing. Cook on medium for 4 hours or low for 7-8 hours.

Crock Pot Orange Chicken

2 lbs. boneless skinless
chicken breasts
2/3 c. all-purpose flour
2/3 c. orange marmalade
1/2 c. mustard
1/2 c. ketchup

2 T. rice wine vinegar
2 T. soy sauce
2 T. brown sugar
1 T. finely grated fresh
ginger
3 scallions, chopped

Spray crockpot with cooking spray. Cut up chicken into bite sized pieces. Sprinkle flour over chicken and toss to coat. Place in crock pot. In separate bowl, mix together remaining ingredients and pour over chicken. Cook on LOW 4-5 hours Serve over rice with fresh steamed broccoli or pea pods.

Dad's BBQ Ribs

Select ribs with moderate amount of fat. Allow about one pound of ribs per person.
Marinade
1 c. Kraft Classis Ranch
Dressing
¼ c. apple cider vinegar

¼ c. soy sauce
1 T. lemon juice

Use large plastic bag or flat pan to marinade ribs. Marinade for a minimum of four hours. Set grill to medium heat and cook ribs about 10 minutes per side to brown them. Then reduce heat to maintain a grill temperature of 225-250° and cook for approximately three hours. Do not exceed temperature or ribs will be tough and stringy.

Barbecue Sauce
1 c. of catsup
¼ c. yellow mustard
¼ c. dark brown sugar
¼ c. Worcestershire sauce

3 T. olive oil
3 T. apple cider vinegar
1 T. chili powder
Salt and pepper to taste

Heat oil in a sauce pan. Add other ingredients and bring to a boil. Reduce heat and simmer for about 30 minutes until sauce thickens.

Dijon Chicken Breasts - Grilled

4 chicken breast halves, skinned and boned
½ c. mayonnaise
2 T. Dijon mustard
1-2 T. soy sauce
1-2 T. Worcestershire sauce
½ tsp. garlic powder

Mix mayonnaise, mustard, soy sauce Worcestershire, and garlic powder. Coat chicken breasts well and marinate for 20-30 minutes. Place chicken on greased grill or rack or broiler pan. Grill or broil about 10 minutes on each side until tender, brushing frequently with marinade mixture. This marinade is also excellent on pork chops.

Eye of Round Roast

Eye of round roast
Salt
Pepper
Oil

Salt the meat, let stand overnight. If the roast you are working with weighs over 4 1/2 pounds, cut it in half crosswise before beginning. Salt all sides of the meat evenly (ideally a coarse salt, such as kosher salt or a nice crunchy coarse sea salt.) Wrap the meat in wrap and refrigerate on a plate 18 to 24 hours. Remove meat from refrigerator, and let sit for 30 to 40 minutes at room temperature to lose some of its chill. Remove and discard the plastic wrap. Pat the surfaces lightly with some paper towel to dry off any excess moisture, then rub the surfaces with some oil or spray lightly with cooking spray, and then rub lightly with some ground black or white pepper or a mixture of both.
Start heating the oven to 225°. Sear/brown all sides of the roast in a frying pan (no need for oil in the pan), then put the roast fat side up on a wire rack, either in a baking pan or on a cookie sheet with sides. When the oven has reached 225°, place the prepared roast in the oven and cook to desired doneness. (Medium doneness for a 3 ½ - 4 ½ lb. roast is about 2 ¼ hours. Remove from oven. If you plan on serving it then, while still warm, cover and let rest for 10 to 15 minutes. If you are planning to use it as sandwich meat, then leave uncovered and let cool completely then slice.

Honey Mustard Grilled Chicken

1 cup mayonnaise
4 T. Dijon mustard
2 T. honey

8 boneless, skinless chicken breast halves

Stir mayonnaise, mustard, and honey
Place chicken on grill. Bruch with ½ of sauce. Grill 8-10 minutes. Turn and brush with remaining sauce. Continue grilling 8-10 minutes or until tender.

Honey-Mustard Pork Tenderloin

¾ c. honey
6 T. light brown sugar
6 T. cider vinegar
3 T. Dijon mustard
1 ½ tsp. paprika

4 (3/4 – 1 lb.) pork tenderloins
1 tsp. salt
1 tsp. pepper

Stir together first 5 ingredients until well blended.
Place pork in a greased 15 x 10 in. jellyroll pan; sprinkle evenly with salt and pepper. Pour honey mixture evenly over pork.
Bake at 375° for 20-30 minutes or until a meat thermometer inserted into thickest portion of pork registers 160°, basting occasionally. Remove pork to a wire rack, and let stand 10 minutes before slicing.
Pour pan drippings into a 3-quart saucepan, and cook, stirring often, over medium-high heat until slightly reduced and thickened for sauce.

Hot Chicken Salad

3 – 4 c. diced cooked chicken
1 can cream of chicken soup
2 T. chopped onion
1 c. cooked rice
¼ tsp. salt
¾ c. mayo

½ c. almonds
3 T. lemon juice
3 hard cooked eggs, chopped
1 c. chopped celery
1 small jar pimentos

Mix above ingredients together. Place in a 9 x 12 inch baking greased dish. Top with 2 – 3 cups bran flakes cereal mixed with ¼ cup melted butter. Bake at 350° for 20-25 minutes.

Lemon Curd Pepper Chicken

8 chicken thighs
1 T. salt
1 T. cracked black pepper

4 T. olive oil
½ - 1 c. lemon curd

Season chicken thighs with salt and cracked black pepper. Drizzle olive oil on chicken and wrap tightly in a few layers of aluminum foil. Placing in cooking pan and bake for 4 hours at 275°. When done, combine juices in the foil with lemon curd to make glaze. Take chicken out of foil and finish on the grill. Brush glaze onto chicken while finishing on grill.

Lemon Pepper Shrimp Scampi

1 cup uncooked orzo
2 T. chopped fresh parsley
½ tsp salt, divided
7 tsp. unsalted butter, divided

1 ½ pounds peeled and deveined jumbo shrimp
2 tsp. minced fresh garlic
2 T. fresh lemon juice
¼ tsp freshly ground black pepper

Cook orzo according to package direction, omitting salt and fat. Drain. Place orzo in a medium bowl. Stir in parsley and ¼ tsp. salt; cover and keep warm. While orzo cooks, melt 1 T. butter in a large nonstick skillet over medium-high heat. Sprinkle shrimp with remaining ¼ tsp. salt. Add half of shrimp to pan; sauté 2 minutes or until shrimp are almost done. Transfer shrimp to a plate. Melt 1 tsp butter in pan. Add remaining shrimp to pan; sauté 2 minutes or until almost done. Transfer shrimp to plate. Melt remaining 1 T. butter in pan. Add garlic to pan; cook 30 seconds, stirring constantly. Add shrimp, juice, and pepper to pan; cook 1 minute or until shrimp is done. Be careful not to overcook.

Meat Loaf

1 ½ lbs. ground beef
¾ c. oats
¼ c. chopped onion
1 ½ tsp. salt

¼ tsp. pepper
1 tsp. Worcestershire sauce
1 c. tomato juice
1 egg

Combine all ingredients and pack into an ungreased loaf pan. Bake 350° for 1 hour 15 minutes.

Mediterranean Chicken Breast and Wild Rice

1 lbs. boneless, skinless chicken breasts, lightly pounded
Salt to taste
Black pepper to taste
2 c. wild rice blend
2 tsp. minced garlic

1 small can petite diced tomatoes or ½ cup sun-dried tomatoes
½ c. capers, drained
4 c. water
¾ c. lemon juice
½ c. extra-virgin olive oil

Season chicken with salt and pepper. Place chicken in slow cooker. Add rice, garlic, tomatoes, and capers. Stir well.
Mix water, lemon juice, and oil in small mixing bowl. Pour mixture over rice and chicken. Stir once to coat chicken. Cover; cook on low for 8 hours.

Milanese Chicken

1/3 c. all-purpose flour
2 eggs, beaten
1 1/4 c. plain bread crumbs
2/3 c. grated Parmesan
Kosher salt and freshly ground black pepper
4 (6 to 8-oz.) boneless and skinless chicken breasts, tenderloins removed

2 tsp. dried basil
1 tsp. dried thyme
1/3 c. canola oil

Put an oven rack in the center of the oven. Preheat the oven to 150°. Line a baking sheet with a wire rack. Using 3 wide shallow bowls, add the flour to 1, the eggs to another and to the third bowl combine the bread crumbs, Parmesan cheese, basil, and thyme. On a work surface, put the chicken between 2 pieces of plastic wrap. Using a meat mallet, lightly pound the chicken until approximately 1/4 to 1/2-inch thick. Season the chicken with salt and pepper. Dredge the chicken pieces in the flour to coat lightly, then dip into the beaten eggs, allowing the excess egg to drip off.

Coat the chicken with the bread crumb mixture, pressing gently to adhere. In a large, nonstick sauté pan, heat the canola oil over medium heat. Add 2 pieces of the breaded chicken into the oil and cook until light golden brown, about 3 to 4 minutes on each side. Transfer the chicken to the prepared baking sheet and keep warm in the oven. Repeat with the remaining chicken. Pour balsamic vinaigrette dressing over each chicken breast and heat thoroughly in the oven.

Mom's Spinach Quiche

1 refrigerated pie crust
6 eggs, beaten
1 ¼ c. whole milk
½ tsp. salt
¼ tsp. pepper
1 T. grated onion

Dash of cayenne pepper (optional)
1 c. cheddar cheese
5 pieces cooked bacon, crumbled

½ pkg frozen, chopped spinach (microwave until thawed and squeeze out the liquid)

Bake pie crust for 3 minutes on 375°. Mix together eggs, milk, salt, pepper, onion, and cayenne pepper. On the bottom of the pie crust, put the cheese, bacon, and spinach. Pour egg mixture on top and sprinkle with a little paprika. Bake 375° for 45 minutes or until knife comes out clean.

Mushroom Asiago chicken

1 lb. boneless skinless chicken breasts
Salt and pepper
½ c. all-purpose flour
4 T. unsalted butter
1 lb. sliced mushrooms
½ tsp. salt
3 cloves garlic, minced
½ c. dry white wine or chicken broth

¾ c. low-sodium chicken broth
3 sprigs fresh thyme or ¾ tsp dried thyme leaves
½ c. heavy cream
½ c. shredded Asiago cheese
Parmesan cheese for sprinkling

Cut each chicken breast into thirds by first cutting each breast in half crosswise, then set the thinner half aside. Slice the thicker part of the breast in half horizontally (parallel to the cutting board) to produce 2 more thin cutlets. Cover the chicken breast pieces with a sheet of plastic wrap and pound with a meat mallet or the bottom of a small skillet until all of the pieces are about 1/4" thick. Lightly season each cutlet on both sides with salt and pepper and dredge in flour, shaking off any excess.

Place a large skillet over medium-high heat and melt about 2 Tbsp. unsalted butter. Add as many cutlets as will fit comfortably into the skillet, but be sure not to overcrowd the pan. Sauté for about 5 minutes until golden brown on the first side, then flip and cook for 1 additional minute. Remove the chicken from the skillet to a plate and cover lightly with foil. Repeat with remaining chicken cutlets.

When all of the chicken is cooked, add remaining butter to the skillet along with the mushrooms and 1/2 tsp salt. Cook for 10 minutes, stirring occasionally, until the mushrooms are golden brown and become softened. Add garlic and cook for an additional 2 minutes.

Pour white wine (or 1/2 cup chicken broth) into the skillet and stir to scrape up anything that is sticking to the bottom of the pan. Once the wine has nearly all evaporated, add 3/4 cup chicken broth and thyme. Bring the mixture to a boil, reduce heat to medium and cook for 10–15 minutes at a rapid simmer until the liquid is reduced by half.

Reduce heat to medium-low and stir in heavy cream. Sprinkle the Asiago cheese over the top of the sauce and stir constantly until the cheese melts. Nestle the chicken back into the skillet and allow it to simmer in the sauce just until the chicken is heated through and the sauce has slightly thickened. Sprinkle with a bit of Parmesan cheese and serve right away, either all by itself, or spooned over pasta or mashed potatoes.

Mushroom Meat

1 (10.75 ounce) cans condensed cream of mushroom soup
1 (1 ounce) package dry onion soup mix
½ c. water or low sodium beef broth
3 lbs. pot roast

In a slow cooker, mix cream of mushroom soup, dry onion soup mix and water. Place pot roast in slow cooker and coat with soup mixture. Cook on high setting for 3 to 4 hours, or on Low setting for 8 to 9 hours.

Poppy Seed Chicken

6 chicken breasts halves
A can cream of chicken soup
1 c. sour cream
1 ½ T. lemon juice

1 stack (24) crushed Ritz crackers
½ - 1 stick melted butter
Poppy seeds

Boil chicken until cooked. Debone and cut into bite sized pieces. Combine chicken, soup, sour cream, and lemon juice. Put in 8 x 8" dish and cover with crushed crackers, and sprinkle generously with poppy seeds. Bake at 350° about 30 minutes or until bubbly.

Pork Tenderloin

2/3 c. honey
6 T. light brown sugar
6 T. cider vinegar
3 T. Dijon mustard
1 ½ tsp. paprika

4 (3/4 – 1 lb.) port tenderloins
1 tsp. salt
1 tsp. pepper

Stir together first 5 ingredients until well blended. Place port in a greased 15 10 in. jellyroll pan; sprinkle evenly with salt and pepper. Pour honey mixture evenly over pork. Bake at 375° for 20 – 30 minutes until a meat thermometer inserted into thickest portion of pork registers 160°, basting occasionally. Remove pork to a wire rack, and let stand 10 minutes before slicing. Pour pan drippings into a 3-quart saucepan, and cook, stirring often, over medium-high heat until slightly reduced and thickened for sauce. Serve with buttermilk biscuits.

Potato Soup – Joan

8 slices bacon (cut into small pieces)
1 c. chopped onion
1 c. chopped celery
4 T. flour
1 ¾ c. powdered non-dairy Cremora
5 C. boiling chicken broth

¼ tsp. salt
¼ tsp. white pepper
¼ tsp. garlic powder
1/4 tsp. thyme
¼ tsp. oregano
Parsley flakes
5-6 med. Potatoes, diced and cooked

Combine bacon, celery, onions. Cook in Dutch oven. Blend in flour, cook and stir one minute. Add Cremora and broth all at once, beating with a wire whisk. Increase heat to moderately high. Stir until mixture thickens. Blend in seasonings and the diced potatoes. Heat thoroughly. Keeps several days in the refrigerator. Serves 12.

Pork Chop and Potato Bake – Joan

6 boneless pork chops
Canola oil
Seasoned salt
½ c. milk
½ c. sour cream
¼ c. pepper

1 bag (24 oz.) frozen O'Brian Potatoes (thawed)
1 can cream of celery soup
1 can shredded cheddar cheese
1 can Durkee's fried onion rings

Preheat oven 350°. Brown chops (no flour) in canola oil; season with seasoned salt and set aside. Stir into potatoes the milk, sour cream, celery coup, pepper, 1/3 c. cheese, and ¼ can onion rings. In a 9x13" baking dish, pour potato mixture and arrange pork chops on top. Bake covered for 90 minutes. Top with remainder of cheese and onion rings. Bake 5 more minutes. (Chicken may be substituted for pork chops.) Serves 6.

S & W Baked Spaghetti

(Every Friday night when we were growing up we went to downtown Chattanooga and either ate at the Home Plate Cafeteria or the S & W Cafeteria. We always got our allowance on Friday night. Friday night was special!)

1 ½ lbs. ground chuck   12 oz. spaghetti (cooked)
1 large onion

Brown together the ground chuck and large onion.

Mix the following together:
28 oz. tomatoes   ½ tsp. chili powder
1 can chicken broth (can use   ¼ tsp. sweet basil
2 bouillon cubes with 1 c   1 tsp. crushed red pepper
water)   1T. sugar
1 can tomato paste (8oz)   1 tsp. salt
1/8 tsp. garlic powder   1 tsp. oregano
¼ tsp. cumin seed

Add the above mixture to the ground chuck and onion mix.
Top with 8 oz. sharp grated cheese. Put in a 9 X 13 dish and bake at 300° for 45 minutes. This dish freezes well.

Salmon Patties

1 can pink salmon   ½ c. corn meal
1 egg   2 T. finely chopped onion
½ c. bread crumbs

Combine all ingredients and shape into patties. Fry in 2-3 T. oil until cooked thoroughly and golden brown.

Dill Sauce:
1½ c. fat-free plain Greek   1 T. chopped fresh dill
yogurt   1 tsp. lemon zest
¼ c. Dijon mustard   1 T. fresh lemon juice

Shepherd's Pie with Beef - Cathy

2 lbs. potatoes, such as   1 large egg yolk
russet, peeled and cubed   1/2 c. cream
2 T. sour cream or softened   Salt and black pepper
cream cheese   1 T. extra-virgin olive oil

1 ¾ lbs. ground beef
1 carrot, chopped
1 onion, chopped
2 T. butter
2 T. all-purpose flour
1 c. beef stock or broth

2 tsp. Worcestershire
1/2 c. frozen peas
1 tsp. sweet paprika
2 T. chopped fresh parsley leaves

Boil potatoes in salted water until tender, about 12 minutes. Drain potatoes and pour them into a bowl. Combine sour cream, egg yolk and cream. Add the cream mixture into potatoes and mash until potatoes are almost smooth.

While potatoes boil, preheat a large skillet over medium high heat. Add oil to hot pan with beef. Season meat with salt and pepper. Brown and crumble meat for 3 or 4 minutes. Add chopped carrot and onion to the meat. Cook veggies with meat 5 minutes, stirring frequently. In a second small skillet over medium heat cook butter and flour together 2 minutes. Whisk in broth and Worcestershire sauce. Thicken gravy 1 minute. Add gravy to meat and vegetables. Stir in peas.

Preheat broiler to high. Fill a small rectangular casserole with meat and vegetable mixture. Spoon potatoes over meat evenly. Top potatoes with paprika and broil 6 to 8 inches from the heat until potatoes are evenly browned. Top casserole dish with chopped parsley and serve.

Shepherd's Pie with Ground Turkey - Cathy

1 1/2 pounds peeled and cut Yukon Gold potatoes
2 tsp. unsalted butter
1 tsp. salt
1/4 tsp. black pepper
2 tsp. canola oil
1 1/2 c. finely chopped onions
1 c. finely chopped carrots

1 lb. lean ground turkey
1 tsp. dried rosemary
1 T. tomato paste
3/4 c. low-sodium chicken broth
2/3 c. frozen peas
2 T. coarsely chopped fresh parsley

Preheat oven to 375°. In a large pot, add the potatoes and cover with cold salted water. Bring to a boil over medium-high heat and cook about 20 minutes until potatoes are tender. Drain and mash with the milk, butter, ½ teaspoon of the salt and pepper. For the meat mixture, heat oil in a large skillet over medium-high heat. Cook onions and carrots about 5-10 minutes, until soft. Then cook turkey, breaking the meat with a fork, until browned (about 5 to 7 minutes). Season with rosemary, the remaining 1/2 teaspoon salt and 1/4 teaspoon pepper. Add the tomato paste and chicken broth, then let simmer for 5 minutes. Finally, stir in the peas. Scrape the cooked meat mixture into a 1 1/2-quart baking dish that is ungreased. Top with the mashed potato mixture. Bake for 30 minutes until top is golden brown. Sprinkle with parsley and serve.

Skinny Chicken Pot Pie - Lori

1 (12 oz.) bag steamable frozen mixed vegetables
3 T. all-purpose flour   1/2 c. chopped onion
1/2 tsp. salt   1 can condensed fat free
1/4 tsp/ pepper   cream of chicken soup
1 ¼ c. skim milk   1/4 c. fat free sour cream
4 boneless skinless chicken breasts cooked and cut into pieces
1 box refrigerated pie crust, softened

Directions:
Cook and drain vegetables as directed on the bag.
Heat oven to 375°. In a saucepan, mix flour, salt, pepper, and milk with a wire whisk until blended. Stir in onion. Cook over medium heat 4 to 6 minutes, stirring constantly, until thickened. Stir in soup and sour cream. Add chicken and cooked vegetables; mix well. Cook, stirring frequently until thoroughly heated. Pour into ungreased 2-quart round casserole dish. Unroll pie crust; place over hot filing. Seal edges and flute as you would a pie. Cut slits in several places in crust. Bake 35 - 40 minutes or until crust is golden brown and mixture is bubbly. Let stand 10 minutes before serving.

Slow Cooker Pork Loin

3 lb. pork loin, trimmed and cut little slits all around the pork
1½ tsp. garlic powder   ½ tsp. ground ginger

131

1½ tsp. onion powder
½ tsp. kosher salt
½ tsp. dried thyme
½ tsp. freshly cracked black pepper
2 T. vegetable oil

2 c. chicken broth
2 T. lemon juice
2 T. regular soy sauce
3 T. cornstarch, dissolved in
3 TB water
Salt and pepper to taste

In a small bowl, combine garlic powder, ground ginger, onion powder, salt, thyme, and pepper, whisking to combine. Rub seasoning all over the entire surface of pork loin. Heat oil in a large skillet until very hot. Brown pork loin on all sides. Transfer pork loin to slow cooker. Add chicken broth, lemon juice, and soy sauce. Pour over the pork. Cover and cook on low for 7-8 hours. (If using tenderloins, reduce cook time to about 4 hours.) When finished, baste pork loin and transfer the pork to a plate and keep warm. Pour all the liquid from the slow cooker into a sauce pan. Add dissolved corn starch. Stir well. Cook on medium heat, stirring constantly, until sauce turns thick and gravy-like. Season with additional salt and pepper, if desired.
Serve warm roast with gravy.

Spaghetti Robbs
1 (32 oz.) crushed tomatoes or tomato sauce

2 reg. size cans diced tomatoes
3 pack multi-color bell peppers
1 sweet yellow onions
1 lb. ground beef
1 package Italian sausage
1 tsp. salt

1/2 tsp. Pepper
2 T chili powder
1/2 tsp. crushed red pepper
1 tsp. Natures Seasoning
1 T. Italian Seasoning
2 tsp. rosemary
Bay leaf

Combine ground beef, sausage, onion, garlic, and peppers in a large Dutch oven. Cook and stir until meat is brown and vegetables are tender. Drain grease. Add tomato sauce and tomatoes to beef. Add seasonings. Simmer spaghetti sauce for 1 hour, stirring occasionally. Remove bay leaf.

Spanish Spaghetti with Olives

16 oz. uncooked thin spaghetti
1 T. olive oil
1 cup chopped onion
2 tsp. minced garlic
2 tsp. dried oregano
1 tsp. celery salt
¼ tsp. crushed red pepper
½ tsp. freshly ground black pepper

1 lb. extra-lean ground beef
3 c. lower-sodium marinara sauce
1 c. pimento-stuffed olives, sliced
2 T. capers
½ c. chopped fresh parsley, divided

Cook pasta according to package directions, omitting salt and fat; drain. Heat a large skillet over medium-high heat. Add oil to pan; swirl to coat. Add onion to pan; sauté 4 minutes or until tender. Add garlic; sauté 1 minute. Stir in oregano, celery salt, red pepper, and black pepper. Add ground beef; cook 5 minutes or until beef is browned, stirring to crumble. Stir in marinara sauce, olives, capers, and 3 T. parsley; bring to a boil. Reduce heat, and simmer 15 minutes. Add spaghetti to sauce mixture. Cook 2 minutes or until thoroughly heated. Sprinkle with remaining 1 T. parsley.

Spicy Beef Roast - Cathy

2 (2 ½ – 3 lb.) beef tip or rump roast
1 tsp. minced garlic
3 T. balsamic vinegar
¼ cup soy sauce

2 T. Worcestershire sauce
1 ½ tsp. dry mustard
½ tsp. salt
1 tsp. cracked pepper

Place roasts in slow cooker. Combine vinegar, soy sauce, Worcestershire sauce and mustard. Brush marinade over roasts. Combine cracked, garlic, and salt. Rub over meat. Cool on low for approx. 8 hours.
Option: Can add cut potatoes, onion, and carrots.

Swiss Steak - Mom

2 T. canola oil
1/2 c. all-purpose flour
1 tsp. salt
½ tsp. pepper
Paprika to taste
4 lbs. beef cube steaks
2 (14.5 ounce) cans crushed tomatoes (may add another can)

2 green bell pepper, sliced into rings
2 red bell pepper, sliced into rings
1 onion, sliced into rings

Heat the oil in a skillet over medium heat. In a bowl, mix the flour, salt and pepper, and paprika. Dredge the steaks in the flour mixture, and place in the skillet. Brown steaks on both sides, and remove from heat. In a slow cooker, alternate layers of steak, green bell pepper, red bell pepper, onion, and tomatoes. Cover, and cook 6 to 8 hours on Low, until steaks are very tender.

Turkey Burgers

1 lb. ground turkey
¼ c. panko bread crumbs
¼ c. shredded sweet onion
2 egg whites, lightly beaten
½ c. fresh baby spinach, chopped

1 clove garlic, peeled and minced
1 ¼ tsp. Montreal steak seasoning
1 T. olive oil

In a large bowl, mix ground turkey, panko, onion, egg whites, spinach, garlic, olive oil, and seasoning. Form into 6 patties. Cook the patties in medium skillet over medium heat, turning once, until they reach an internal temperature of 180° or cook in a George Foreman grill.

Best Ever Blueberry Muffins- Cathy

1 1/2 cups all-purpose flour
(You can use a mix of white
and wheat flour.)
3/4 c. white sugar
1/2 tsp. salt
2 tsp. baking powder
1/3 c. canola or coconut oil
1 egg

1/3 c. milk
1 c. fresh or frozen
blueberries
3 T. white sugar
1 T. all-purpose flour
1 ½ T. butter, cubed
1/2 tsp. ground cinnamon

Preheat oven to 400°. Grease muffin cups or line with muffin liners. Combine 1 1/2 cups flour, 3/4 cup sugar, salt and baking powder. Place oil into a 1 cup measuring cup; add the egg and enough milk to fill the cup. Mix this with flour mixture. Fold in blueberries. Fill muffin cups right to the top, and sprinkle with crumb topping mixture.

To Make Crumb Topping: Mix together 1/4 cup sugar, 2T. flour,1 T. butter, and ½ tsp. cinnamon. Mix with fork, and sprinkle over muffins before baking. Bake for 20 to 25 minutes in the preheated oven, or until done.

Best-Ever Scones - Cathy

2 c. all-purpose flour
1/3 c. sugar
1 T. baking powder
1/2 tsp. salt

1/2 c. cold butter, cut into
1/2-inch cubes
1 c. whipping cream, divided

Preheat oven to 450°. Stir together first 4 ingredients in a large bowl. Cut butter into flour mixture with a pastry blender until crumbly and mixture resembles small peas. Freeze 5 minutes. Add 3/4 cup plus 2 Tbsp. cream, stirring just until dry ingredients are moistened. Turn dough out onto wax paper; gently press or pat dough into a 7-inch round (mixture will be crumbly). Cut round into 8 wedges. Place wedges 2 inches apart on a lightly greased baking sheet. Brush tops of wedges with remaining 2 Tbsp. cream just until

Bread Machine Focaccia Bread - Cathy

1 c. lukewarm water
2 T. olive oil
½ tsp. salt
2 tsp. chopped garlic
1 T. chopped fresh

3 c. bread flour
1 ½ tsp. active dry yeast
2 T. olive oil
Rosemary

Place water, 2 tablespoons olive oil, salt, garlic, 1 tablespoon rosemary, bread flour and yeast in the pan of the bread machine in the order recommended by the manufacturer. Select dough cycle; press start. Remove dough from bread machine when cycle is complete. Pat dough into either a 9x13 inch baking pan or 12 inch pizza pan. Use your fingers to dimple the dough every inch or so. Brush with remaining olive oil and sprinkle with remaining rosemary. Preheat oven to 400°. Cover focaccia with plastic wrap while oven preheats. Bake in preheated oven for 20 to 25 minutes, or until golden brown. Let cool for 5 minutes before serving.

Bread Machine Whole Wheat Bread

1 egg
1 c. water (between 120-140 degrees)
2 T. olive oil
1/3 c. honey

3 1/3 c. whole wheat flour
2 tsp. yeast (one package rapid rise)
1 1/2 tsp. salt

Put the dough paddle in the bread machine pan. Place ingredients in the order listed above. Crack egg into bowl, then pour into pan. Make a well in the center of the flour. Place yeast and salt in the well. Place your bread machine on the whole wheat cycle or according to your bread machine's instructions. I choose "light" crust because it's easier to slice.

Butter Brickle Bread

1 box yellow cake mix
1 small box French Vanilla pudding
4 large eggs
½ c. oil or applesauce
½ tsp. vanilla
1 c. almond brickle chips or toffee chips
1 c. toasted pecans

Preheat oven to 350°. Combine mix and next 5 ingredients. Beat at medium for 5 minutes. Stir in chips. Spray 2 medium loaf pans. Sprinkle pecans in pans. Pour in batter. Bake 350° for approx. 50 minutes. Cool on wire rack for 10 minutes.

Buttery Bread Machine Rolls

1 c. warm milk (70 to 80 degrees F.)
1/2 c. butter, softened
1/4 c. sugar
2 eggs
1 1/2 tsp. salt
4 c. bread flour
2 1/4 tsp. active dry yeast

In bread machine pan, put all ingredients in order suggested by manufacturer. Select dough setting. When cycle is completed, turn dough onto a lightly floured surface. Spread into a rectangle in a 13 x 9 inch baking pan. OR divide dough into 24 portions and shape dough into balls. Cover and let rise in a warm place for 30-45 minutes. Bake at 350° for 13-16 minutes or until golden brown.

Cheddar Cheese Bread

3 c. flour
1 T. baking powder
1 tsp. salt
1/4 tsp. cayenne pepper
1/8 tsp. black pepper
4 oz. shredded sharp cheddar cheese
1 1/4 c. milk
3/4 c. sour cream
3 T. of butter, melted
1 egg, lightly beaten
Topping
1/4 c. shredded sharp Cheddar cheese (1 oz)
1 T. butter or margarine, cut into pieces

Heat oven to 350°. Grease a 9×5 loaf pan with oil. In a bowl, whisk together the first 5 ingredients. Carefully stir in cheese until covered in flour mixture, this will help prevent your cheese sinking to the bottom of your loaf of bread. In a different bowl, whisk together the remaining ingredients. Fold the wet mixture into the flour and cheese mixture, stir until just combined, do not over stir. Spread the mixture into the loaf pan. Sprinkle with 1/4 cup cheese. Top with 1 tablespoon butter. Bake for 45-50 minutes. Let cool 10 minutes and then remove from pan. Allow to cool for one hour before slicing and serving. Wrap tightly and store at room temperature up to 4 days, or refrigerate up to 10 days.

Cheese Bread (an Easter staple)

3 ½ c. Bisquick
2 ½ c. shredded cheese
1 – 3 tsp. diced onion
1 ¼ c. milk

¼ tsp. garlic powder
¼ tsp. salt
2 eggs

Mix Bisquick, cheese and seasoning. Add milk and egg. Mix until moist. Preheat oven to 350°. Pour into greased loaf pan. Sprinkle with some g rated cheese and dot with butter. Bake until done, 45 to 50 minutes. Should be brown and crusty on top.

Cornbread Muffins

1 ¾ c. flour
1 c. yellow corn meal
1/3 c. sugar
1 tsp. salt
¼ t. baking soda

2 tsp. baking powder
1 ¼ c. milk
¼ c. canola oil
1 egg, lightly beaten

Preheat oven to 400°. Combine dry ingredients. Stir in wet ingredients until moistened. Fill 12 muffin tins ¾ full. Bake 20-35 minutes.

Cranberry Bread

2 c. all-purpose flour
½ tsp. salt
1 ½ tsp baking powder
½ tsp. baking soda
1 c. sugar
1 egg, well beaten
2 T. melted butter

2 T. hot water
½ c. orange juice
¼ c. grated orange rind
1 c. fresh or dried cranberries
½ c. chopped nuts

Preheat oven to 325°. Grease a 9 x 5 inch loaf pan or 3 mini loaf pans. Combine flour, salt, baking powder, and baking soda. Add sugar, egg, butter, hot water, orange juice, and grated orange rind; stir until moistened. Fold in berries and nuts. Spoon into pan and bake 50 minutes (or 35 minutes for mini loaves). Cool; wrap and refrigerate or freeze.

Garlic Biscuits

2 c. Bisquick baking mix
$^{1}/_{2}$ c. cold water
$^{3}/_{4}$ c. shredded sharp cheddar cheese

$^{1}/_{4}$ c. butter
1 tsp. dried parsley
$^{1}/_{2}$ tsp. garlic powder
$^{1}/_{2}$ tsp. Italian seasoning

Heat oven to 450°. Combine baking mix, water and grated cheese in a bowl. Roll out on a lightly floured surface, until 1 inch thick. Cut biscuits, and place on an ungreased pan.
Melt butter and spices together. Brush the biscuits with the butter and bake for 8 to 10 minutes.

Homemade Dinner Rolls- Mom

1 pkg. quick-acting active dry yeast
1 1/3 c. milk (105° to 115°F degrees)
3 to 3 1/2 c. flour or whole wheat flour

3 T. olive oil
1 T. sugar
1 tsp. salt
1 T. melted butter
Coarse salt

Dissolve yeast in warm milk with sugar in electric mixer bowl. Stir in 1 cup flour, oil, and salt. Beat until smooth. Stir in enough remaining flour, scraping dough from side of bowl, until soft dough forms. Cover and let rise in warm place until double, about 45 minutes. Heat oven 400°. Prep a 12 cup muffin pan with non-stick cooking spray. Punch down dough in center and fold over a few times. Pinch off 1 inch balls of dough and quickly roll in palm of hands. Put 3 balls to one muffin cup; brush with melted butter; sprinkle with coarse salt. Bake 12 to 15 minutes, until crust is light golden brown. Immediately remove from pan. Store loosely covered.

Buttermilk Biscuits

1 c. butter
4 c. self-rising flour

1 ½ c. buttermilk
¼ c. butter, melted

Cut 1 c. butter into flour with a pastry blender or fork until crumbly; add buttermilk, stirring until dry ingredients are moistened. Turn dough out onto a lightly floured surface; knead 3 to 5 times. Pat or roll dough to ½ in. thickness, and cut with a 2 in. round cutter. Place dough on lightly greased baking sheets. Reroll excess dough, and proceed as directed. Bake at 425° for 10-13 minutes or until golden. Brush with ¼ cup melted butter.

Italian Herb Bread- Cathy

1 ¼ c. water
1 ½ T. olive oil
1 tsp. salt
3 ½ c. bread flour
2 tsp. sugar
1 T. dried parsley

2 tsp. dried onion flakes
½ tsp. dried basil
1 tsp. Italian herbs
½ tsp. garlic powder
2 tsp. active dry yeast

Measure and add liquid ingredients to the bread pan. Measure and add dry ingredients (except yeast) to the bread pan. Use your finger to form a well in the flour where you will pour the yeast. Don't let the yeast come into contact with a liquid when you are adding ingredients. Measure the yeast and carefully pour it into the well. Snap the baking pan into the bread maker and close the lid. Select the French setting and the crust of your choice. Press the start button.

Overnight Blueberry French Toast

12 slices day-old Italian bread, cut into 1-inch cubes

1 ½ (8 ounce) packages cream cheese, cut into 1 inch cubes

2 c. fresh blueberries

10 eggs, beaten

¼ c. powdered sugar

2 c. milk

1 tsp. vanilla extract

Cinnamon

1/3 c. maple syrup

1 ½ c. white sugar

3 tablespoons cornstarch

1 ½ c. water

1 T. lemon juice

1 ½ cup fresh blueberries

1 T. butter

Lightly grease a 9x13in baking dish. Arrange half the bread cubes in the dish. Sprinkle with cinnamon. Mix cream cheese, powdered sugar, and some milk and spread on top of bread. Sprinkle 2 cups blueberries over the cream cheese and top with remaining bread cubes. Remove the bread mixture from the refrigerator about 30 minutes before baking. Preheat the oven to 350°. Cover, and bake 30 minutes. Uncover, and continue baking 25 to 30 minutes until center is firm and surface is lightly browned. In a medium saucepan, mix the sugar, cornstarch, and water. Bring to a boil. Stirring constantly, cook 3 to 4 minutes. Mix in the remaining 1 cup blueberries. Reduce heat, and simmer 10 minutes, until the blueberries burst. Stir in the butter, and pour ½ over the baked French toast and serve. Serve the remaining syrup on the side.

Sour Cream Rolls – a favorite among the grandchildren

½ stick melted butter
1 c. Bisquick

½ c. sour cream

Mix together and put into muffin tin Bake on 400° for 10 – 12 minutes.

Whole Wheat Blueberry Scones - Cathy

2 ½ c. whole wheat flour
2 tsp. baking powder
½ tsp. salt
½ tsp. baking soda
¼ c. brown sugar (dark or light)
¼ c. sugar or sugar substitute
4 T. cold butter, cut into small pieces

2/3 c. buttermilk (may need to add more)
1 egg
1 tsp. high quality vanilla extract
1 c. frozen blueberries tossed in 1 tsp. flour
(Walnuts, cranberries, optional)
½ c. rolled oats

Preheat oven to 400°. Line a baking sheet with a Silpat, with parchment, or spray with cooking spray. You can also use a scone pan. In a medium bowl, whisk together the flour, baking powder, baking soda, salt, and brown sugar.
Cut the butter into the flour mixture using a pastry blender, two knives, or your fingers. In a small bowl, whisk together the milk, the egg, and the vanilla extract. Add the liquid mixture to the flour-butter mixture, and stir until just combined. Stir in the blueberries. Add walnuts and cranberries if desired. Spread ¼ rolled oats in the bottom of the baking sheet. Gather the dough mixture together into a round disk and place on top of the oats. Pat the disk out to about ½ inch thickness and press down into the oats. Spread the remaining oats on top. Cut the dough into as many scones as you want. 8 for large scones or 16 for small ones. Bake the scones for approx. 15 minutes based on your oven and the scone size. Serve with orange marmalade, lemon curd, or Devon cream.

DESSERTS

Apple Crumb Cake - Lori

For the crumb topping:
½ cup all-purpose flour
¼ cup butter
½ cup light brown sugar
¼ t salt
2 t cinnamon

For the cake:
1½ cups flour
½ t baking soda
1 ¼ t cinnamon
¼ t nutmeg
¼ t salt
2/3 cup vegetable oil
¾ cups sugar
¼ cup brown sugar
1 egg
1 egg white
1 t vanilla
1 large apple, peeled and cut into small pieces
¾ cup chopped walnuts

Glaze:
1½ tablespoons butter, melted
1½ tablespoons brown sugar
1½ tablespoons sugar
1½ tablespoons milk
¼ teaspoon vanilla
¾ cup powdered sugar

Preheat oven 350°. Spray 9X9 pan with cooking spray. Set aside. Make the crumb topping first. In a small bowl, toss the flour, brown sugar, salt and cinnamon together. Cut in the butter. Mix to create crumbs. Set aside.
Sift together flour, baking soda, cinnamon, nutmeg, and salt. Sift again and set aside. In a medium bowl, whisk the oil, sugar, brown sugar, egg, egg white, and vanilla together until combined. Pour the wet ingredients into the dry ingredients and stir until almost combined. Don't overmix. The batter will be very thick. Fold in apples and walnuts and mix until combined. Pour the batter in the prepared baking pan. Speak to make an even surface. Pour the crumb topping evenly on top and gently press them down into the batter. Bake the cake for 30-35 minutes. If the cake jiggles in the middle, bake for 5 more minutes. To make the glaze, whisk the melted butter, brown sugar, white sugar, milk, and vanilla together in a small bowl. Add the powdered sugar and whisk until just combined. Drizzle over the cake.

Apple Pie

3 Granny Smith apples, sliced
½ c. sugar
1 tsp. cinnamon
1 refrigerator pie crust

Topping:
½ c. sugar
¾ c. flour
1 stick of cold butter

Place crust in pie pan. Fill crust with apples. Top apples with sugar and cinnamon and stir to make sure that all apples are covered. In a separate bowl, mix sugar and flour, then crumble butter and cut it in with a fork. Place on top of apples. Bake at 400° for 50 minutes.

Apple Crisp

6 sliced apples
¾ tsp. cinnamon
¼ tsp. nutmeg
1 T. water
2 tsp. lemon juice

½ c. sugar
½ c. oats
½ c. brown sugar
½ c. flour
¾ stick butter

Mix in large bowl. Then place in buttered square baking dish. Top with the following.

½ c. sugar
½ c. oats
½ c. brown sugar

½ c. flour
¾ stick butter

Cut with pastry blender. Sprinkle on top of apples. Bake 350° for 40 minutes.

Barbara Bush Oatmeal Chip Cookies

1 c. butter
1 c. sugar
1 c. brown sugar
2 eggs
2 c. flour
1 tsp. baking soda

1 tsp. salt
2 c. quick-cooking rolled oats
2 tsp. vanilla
1 (12 oz.) pkg. chocolate chips

Blend butter and sugars until fluffy. Beat in eggs. Sift flour, baking soda and salt; add to butter mixture. Stir in oats, vanilla and chips. Drop by tablespoon onto a greased cookie sheet. Bake at 350° for 8-10 minutes or until golden. Makes about 6 doz.cookies.

Best Ever Brownies - Cathy

Heat oven to 350°. Grease a 9-inch square pan.
Whisk the following dry ingredients in a bowl:

1 c. flour
½ tsp. salt
¾ c. cocoa
1 ½ c. sugar
½ c. brown sugar

½ c. walnuts
¼ c. white semi-sweet choc. chips
¼ c. semi-sweet choc. chips

Stir in the following:
½ c. melted butter   ½ tsp. vanilla.
3 eggs, beaten
Spread into pan. Bake until toothpick inserted in center has a few crumbs, approx. 35 minutes. Cool. Makes 12.
*(I use Watkins Pure Vanilla Extract.)

Blueberry Crunch – Joan

Pour 1 can crushed pineapple (20 oz.) into 13x9" baking pan. On top of it pour 1 can blueberry pie filling. Sprinkle 1 box butter recipe yellow cake mix on top of above. Sprinkle 1 can chopped pecans on top. Pour ¾ c. melted. Bake at 350° for 35-40 minutes.

Brabson House Cajun Cake

(This is from our local favorite tea room years ago.)
2 c. flour   3 eggs
2 c. sugar   1 tsp. cinnamon
4 T. cocoa   1 tsp. soda
1 c. water   1 tsp. vanilla
2 sticks butter   ½ c. buttermilk

Sift flour and sugar. Place butter, cocoa, water in pan and boil. Pour over flour. Beat well. Add buttermilk, soda, cinnamon, and eggs. Mix. Pour in greased and floured 9 x 15 pan. Bake 350°. 20-25 min.
Icing:
6 T. heavy cream   4 T. cocoa
1 stick butter   1 lb. xxx sugar

1 tsp. vanilla
Melt butter. Add other ingredients. Beat. Pour over hot cake.

Bread Pudding - Mom

7 or 8 slices of cubed Italian or Challah bread (day old is best)

2/3 c. sugar	½ tsp. cinnamon
2 large beaten eggs	½ tsp. nutmeg
3 c. milk	¼ tsp. baking powder
1 T. butter	¼ tsp. salt
2 tsp. vanilla extract	½ c. raisins, optional

Coat 8 x 12 inch casserole dish with butter. Cut bread into ¾ in. pieces and put aside. Combine remaining ingredients and mix well. Add the bread (and raisins) and mix well. Add to casserole dish and sprinkle with nutmeg. Bake in 350° oven for 45 minutes.

Bread Pudding - Cathy

Unsalted butter, softened	4 c. milk
1 (1 ½ -lb. loaf cinnamon	2 c. heavy whipping cream
egg bread	¼ c. vanilla extract
2/3 c. golden raisins	8 eggs, beaten
1 ½ c. sugar	1 tsp. cinnamon

Coat the bottom and side of a 2 in. deep baking dish heavily with butter. Tear the bread into 1 in. pieces. Mix with the raisins in a bowl. Spread the bread mixture evenly in the prepared dish. Turning crust side down as this tends to burn easily. Whisk the sugar, milk, whipping cream, vanilla, eggs, and cinnamon in a bowl until blended. Pour over the bread mixture. Preheat the oven to 325°. Place the baking dish in a 4 in. deep baking pan. Add water to reach halfway up the side of th4e baking dish. Bake 1 hour. Remove from water bath. Let stand 20 minutes. Serve warm.

Carrot Cake- Mom

2 c. all-purpose flour
2 tsp. baking soda
1/2 tsp. salt
2 tsp. ground cinnamon
3 large eggs
2 c. sugar
3/4 c. canola oil
3/4 c. buttermilk

2 tsp. vanilla extract
2 c. grated carrot
1 (8-ounce) can crushed
pineapple, drained
1 (3 1/2-ounce) can flaked
coconut
1 c. chopped pecans or
walnuts

Line 3 (9-inch) round cake pans with wax paper; lightly grease and flour wax paper. Set pans aside. Stir together first 4 ingredients. Beat eggs and next 4 ingredients at medium speed with an electric mixer until smooth. Add flour mixture, beating at low speed until blended. Fold in carrot and next 3 ingredients. Pour batter into prepared cake pans. Bake at 350° for 25 to 30 minutes or until a wooden pick inserted in center comes out clean. Cool in pans on wire racks 15 minutes. Remove from pans, and cool completely on wire racks. Spread Cream Cheese Frosting between layers and on top and sides of cake.

Cream Cheese Frosting
3/4 cup butter or margarine, softened
1 (8-ounce) package cream cheese, softened
1 (3-ounce) package cream cheese, softened
3 cups sifted powdered sugar
1 1/2 teaspoons vanilla extract
Beat butter and cream cheese at medium speed with an electric mixer until creamy. Add powdered sugar and vanilla; beat until smooth.

Chart House Mud Pie

½ pkg. chocolate wafer
cookies
¼ c. butter, melted

1 gallon coffee ice cream
1 ½ c. fudge sauce

Crush wafers and add butter. Mix well. Press into a 9" pie pan. Cover with soft coffee ice cream. Top with cold fudge sauce. (It helps to place fudge sauce in the freezer for a while to make spreading easier.) Store the Mud Pie in the freezer for approx. 10 hours. Slice the pie into eight portions and serve on chilled dessert plates. Top with whipped cream and diced almonds.

Cherry Crisp

1 can cherry pie filling
2/3 c. packed brown sugar
½ c. all-purpose flour
½ c. oats

¾ tsp. cinnamon
¾ tsp. nutmeg
1/3 c. softened butter

Heat oven to 375°. Grease square 8x8x2 pan. Place cherries in pan. Mix remaining ingredients and sprinkle over cherries. Bake 30 min. 6 servings.

Cherry Pie

Pastry for 9-inch two-crust pie
1 1/3 c. sugar
1/3 c. all-purpose flour
2 cans pitted red tart
cherries, drained

¼ tsp. almond extract
3 T. butter

Heat oven to 425°. Place pastry in pie pan. Stir together sugar and flour; mix with cherries. Pour into pie pan; sprinkle with almond extract and dot with butter. Cover with top crust which has slits cut in it; seal and flute the edges. Cover edge with 2- to 3-inch strip of aluminum foil to prevent excessive browning; remove foil last 15 minutes of baking. Bake 35 to 45 minutes or until crust is brown and juice begins to bubble through slits in crust.

Chocolate Chip Cheese Cake – Mom

Crust-
2 ½ c. graham cracker crumbs
3 T. sugar
1/3 c. melted butter (may need a little more)
Combine and press firmly and evenly on bottom and sides of spring form pan which has been sprayed with baking spray. Press down with measuring cup. Chill for 30 minutes. Prepare filling.

3 (8 oz.) pkgs. cream cheese, room temperature
1 c. sugar   1 T. lemon juice
3 eggs, room temperature   ½ tsp. vanilla

Beat cheese and sugar until light and fluffy. Add eggs 1 at a time. Blend well after each. Blend in lemon juice and vanilla. Stir in ½ c. mini semi-sweet chocolate chips. Pour into chilled crust. Bake 350-375° for 40 minutes. Carefully remove from oven. Cool for at least 30 minutes. Then spread with chocolate topping: Melt 1/3 c. mini chocolate chips and 2 T. whipping cream in microwave on high for 20-30 seconds or just until chips are melted and mixture is smooth when stirred. Cool slightly and spread over top of cheese cake. Refrigerate about 30 minute4s or until topping is set. Cover and refrigerate overnight.

Chocolate Chip Pound Cake – Cathy

1 (18 ¼ oz.) box yellow cake   4 large eggs
mix with pudding   1 (8 oz.) carton sour cream
1 choc. instant pudding mix   ¼ of a (6 oz.) pkg.
½ c. sugar   semisweet chocolate morsels
¾ c. water   Powdered sugar
¾ c. canola oil

Combine cake mix, pudding mix, and sugar. Add oil, water, and eggs. Stir in sour cream and chocolate morsels. Pour batter into greased and floured 12 c. Bundt cake pan. Bake at 350° for 1 hour. Cool in pan for 10 min. Remove from pan and cool completely. Sprinkle with powdered sugar.

Chocolate Fudge Cake and Icing

(From family friend Lena Giffe.)

2 c. plain flour	2 c. sugar
½ - ¾ c. buttermilk	½ oil
3 T. cocoa	2 eggs
1 tsp. soda	1 tsp. vanilla
1 c. water	1 stick butter

Place in saucepan, the butter, cocoa, oil, and water. Bring to a boil for 1 minute, then pour this over the flour and sugar. Beat well. Add eggs, buttermilk, soda, and vanilla. Mix. Pour into greased and floured 9x12x2 inch pan. Bake 350° for 25-30 minutes. When cake is almost done, prepare icing.

Icing:

4 T. cocoa	4 T. milk
1 box confectioners' sugar	1 c. chopped nuts
1 stick butter1 tsp. vanilla	

In saucepan bring to a boil the cocoa, butter, and milk. Remove and add sugar. May need to add bit more milk. Add vanilla and nuts. Mix well. Ice cake as soon as it comes out of oven.

Chocolate Pecan Pie (Paula Deen)

1 (9-inch) unbaked pie shell	1 c. sugar
2 c. pecan halves	2 T. good-quality bourbon
3 large eggs, beaten	3 oz. semisweet chocolate,
3 T. butter, melted	chopped
1/2 c. dark corn syrup	

Preheat the oven to 375°. Cover bottom of pie crust with pecans. In a medium bowl, whisk together the eggs and melted butter. Add the corn syrup, sugar, bourbon and the chopped chocolate. Stir until all ingredients are combined. Pour mixture into the pie shell over the pecans and place on a heavy-duty cookie sheet. Bake for 10 minutes. Lower the oven temperature to 350° and continue to bake for an additional 25 minutes or until pie is set. Remove from oven and cool on a wire rack.

Chocolate Pound Cake – Mom

(Mom takes this cake to the Lee Family reunion every year.)

1 c. butter	½ c. cocoa
1 c. vegetable shortening	½ tsp. baking powder
3 c. sugar	1 tsp. salt
5 eggs	1 ¼ c. milk
3 c. all-purpose flour	1 tsp. vanilla

1 (1-az.) square unsweetened chocolate, grated

In a large mixer bowl cream butter, shortening and sugar until light and fluffy, about 5 minutes. Add eggs, 1 at a time, beating after each addition. Sift dry ingredients together. Add to creamed mixture alternately with milk at low speed. Add vanilla and grated chocolate. Pour into a greased and floured 10" tube pan. Bake at 350° for 1 hour and 30 minutes, or until cake tests done. Let cool in pan 10 minutes before removing. Glaze, if desired, with the following glaze.

2 T. cocoa	1 T. butter
2 T. water	½ tsp. vanilla
1 T. white corn syrup	1 c. confectioners' sugar

Combine in a saucepan cocoa, water, corn syrup, and water. Add vanilla and confectioners' sugar. Spread over warm cake.

Chocolate Strawberry Nutella Cake

Cake

2 sticks Butter
4 T. (heaping) cocoa powder
1 c. boiling water
2 c. flour
2 c. sugar
¼ tsp. salt
½ c. buttermilk
2 whole eggs

1 tsp. baking soda
1 tsp. vanilla
1-½ c. Nutella
2 pints Strawberries, hulled
and sliced
¼ c. sugar
1 tsp. vanilla

Whipped cream
2 c. heavy cream
½ c. powdered sugar

Preheat the oven to 350° degrees. Line 2 round baking pans with parchment, then spray the parchment with baking spray. In a medium saucepan, melt the butter. Add the cocoa and stir it until smooth. Pour in the boiling water, let the mixture bubble up for 20 seconds or so, then turn it off and set it aside. In a measuring pitcher or bowl, mix together the buttermilk, baking soda, eggs, and vanilla. Set aside. In a large mixing bowl, mix together the sugar, flour, and salt. Stir in the hot chocolate mixture, stirring gently until it's halfway combined and less hot. Pour in the buttermilk mixture and continue stirring gently until the batter is all combined. Pour the batter into the pans and bake them for 17-20 minute, until they're just set. Remove them from the pans and set them aside to cool completely.

Meanwhile, prepare the strawberries by stirring them with the sugar and the vanilla. Let them macerate for 15 minutes, then drain off the excess juice. Whip the cream with the powdered sugar. To assemble, turn one layer upside down on a serving platter. Spread half the Nutella all over the surface. Spread on half the whipped cream and top with half the strawberries Place the other layer upside down on top and repeat with the rest of the Nutella, whipped cream, and strawberries. Keep chilled until serving. Cut with a serrated knife!

Note: Don't assemble more than an hour before serving.

Chocolate Swirl Cheesecake- Mom

12 oz. cream cheese, softened
½ c. sugar
1 t. lemon grated lemon rind
2 eggs
1 ½ c. sour cream
2/3 c. (4 oz) semisweet chocolate morsels, melted
Chocolate Crumb crust

Combine first 3 ingredients in a medium bowl. Beat at medium speed until smooth and well blended. Add eggs one at a time, beating after each addition. Add sour cream and beat until thoroughly mixed. Combine 1 cup cheese cake mixture and melted chocolate and set aside. Pour remaining cheese cake mixture into crust. Pour chocolate mixture over cheese cake mixture, gently swirling with a knife. Bake at 325° for 30 to 35 minutes. Cool on a rack for 1 to 2 hours; chill 8 hours.
Chocolate Crumb crust
1 ½ c. chocolate chip cookie crumbs
½ tsp. ground cinnamon
¼ c. butter, melted
Combine all ingredients. Press firmly into bottom of a greased 8" spring-form pan and chill.

Chocolate Wafer Pie- Mom

¾ c. chocolate wafer crumbs
3 eggs, separated
¼ tsp. salt
¾ c. sugar
¾ c. chopped pecans
1 tsp. vanilla
½ pt. whipping cream

Roll wafers; add salt, separate eggs. Beat egg whites until stiff; continue beating adding sugar (1 tablespoon at a time) until shiny stiff peaks appear. Add vanilla, mix well. Add wafer crumbs and nuts folding into mixture. Grease pie plate with butter. Spread evenly on bottom and sides. Bake at 350° for 30 minutes. Cool.
Topping for Chocolate Wafer Pie:
½ pt. whipping cream   1 tsp. vanilla
Whip together and spread on cooled pie. Grate small amount of chocolate bar on top.

Coconut Layer Cake

2 ½ c. sifted flour
3 tsp. baking powder
½ tsp. salt
½ cup softened shortening
1 1/3 c. sugar
1 c. milk

1 tsp. vanilla
2 tsp. coconut flavoring
1 c. grated fresh coconut, or
1 can (3 ½ oz.) flaked
coconut
4 egg whites

Coconut frosting

Preheat oven to 350 degrees. Lightly grease, then kine with waxed paper bottoms of two 8" (2" deep) cake pans. Sift flour with baking powder and salt; set aside. In a large bowl at medium speed beat shortening until creamy. Gradually add 1 C. sugar, beating until very light and fluffy. At low speed beat in flour mixture, alternating with milk, beginning and ending with flour. Beat only until combined. Stir in vanilla, coconut flavoring and coconut.

In medium bowl beat egg whites, using a rotary or hand electric mixer, beat egg whites just until soft peaks form when beater is slowly raised. Gradually add rest of sugar, beating until stiff peaks form. With rubber scraper, gently fold egg whites into batter, using an under and over motion, until well combined. Turn into pans; bake 25 to 30 minutes, or until surface of cake springs back when gently depressed with fingertip.

Let cool 10 minutes then gently remove from pans. Cool completely on wire rack.

Coconut Frosting

2 egg whites
1 ½ C. sugar
¼ t. cream of tartar

1 T. light corn syrup
½ t. vanilla extract
½ t. coconut flavoring

2 ½ C. grated coconut or 2 cans (3 ½ oz size) flaked coconut
Combine egg whites, sugar, cream of tartar and corn syrup with 6 T. water in top of double boiler. Cook over boiling water, beating constantly with hand mixer at high speed until mixture stands at high peaks when beater is slowly raised. Stir in vanilla and coconut flavoring and use to fill and frost cake. Sprinkle fresh coconut on frosting.

Coconut Logs- Mom

1 ½ stick butter
1 c. sugar
1 c. dates, cut up

2 c. rice krispies
½ c. chopped walnuts
1 egg

Combine butter, sugar, dates, and egg in saucepan. Boil 6 minutes, stirring constantly. Remove from heat. Add rice crispies and walnuts. Put in 8 x 8 square pan. Cut into small rectangles. Roll in coconut, shaping into a log. Place on wax paper. Note: These will be real buttery but when cool will thicken.

Cream Cheese Key Lime Pie- Cathy

1 (8 oz.) package cream cheese
1 can sweet condensed milk
½ c. lime juice

2 egg yolks
1 tsp. vanilla
1 T. sugar

Mix and pour in prepared graham cracker crust.
Graham Cracker Crust

1 ¼ c. graham cracker crumbs

1/3 c. melted butter
3 T. sugar

Mix. Press into 9 in. pie pan. Bake 8 minutes at 350° degrees. Let cool before filling.
Whipped Cream Topping
Mix ½ pint heavy whipping cream with 4 T. powdered sugar and ½ tsp. vanilla until stiff peaks form. Spread over cream cheese filling. Refrigerate 5-6 hours.

Easy Fresh Peach Cobbler- Nana Robbs

2 c. peaches, peeled and sliced
½ c. sugar
1 stick butter
½ c. milk

1 c. sifted plain flour
1/1/2 tsp. baking powder
1 c. sugar
Pinch of salt

Mix peaches with ½ c. sugar. Set stand for 30 minutes or till juice forms. Melt butter in 2 qt. baking dish. Make batter of remaining ingredients. Pour batter over butter then pour fruit and juice over batter. Do not stir. Bake at 350° for 30–45 minutes. Other fruits may be substituted. Serves 8-10.

Easy Pound Cake- Mom

2 sticks of margarine
11/2 c. sugar
6 eggs

2 c. all-purpose flour
1 tsp. vanilla flavoring
¼ tsp. lemon flavoring

Mix margarine and sugar and alternate eggs and flour. Add flavoring. Bake at 325° for one hour starting in a cold oven.

Fehn's Macaroon Pie

(Fehn's was one of our favorite restaurants!)

18 soda crackers
1 c. sugar
½ tsp. baking powder
12 dates, chopped
½ to 1 c. chopped pecans or

walnuts
1 tsp. almond or vanilla
extract, or ½ and ½
3 egg whites

Roll crackers until finely ground. Add sugar, baking powder, dates, pecans and extract. Beat egg whites until stiff and fold in. Put in well-greased pan and bake at 350 for 25-30 minutes. Let cool in pie plate on a rack; pie will sink a bit and be crispy on the outside and chewy on the inside.
Serve with whipped cream, ice cream, or plain.

French Coconut Pie - Lori

3 large eggs, beaten
1 ½ c. sugar
1 c. flaked coconut
1 stick melted butter

1 T. white vinegar
1 tsp. vanilla
Pinch of salt
9" refrigerated pie shell

Mix everything together and pour into the pie shell. Bake at 350° for 1 hour. Let cool before slicing. Serve with homemade whipping cream.

Fudge Pie- Mom

(This pie has been our "go to" pie for years because we always have ingredients on hand.)

1 stick butter	2 eggs
1 c. sugar	1 tsp. vanilla
3 ½ T. cocoa	½ c. chopped pecans
¼ c. flour	(optional)
Pinch of salt	

Melt butter in saucepan. In separate bowl combine dry ingredients: sugar, cocoa, flour, and salt. Add to butter. Add 2 eggs, slightly beaten, and vanilla. Add pecans.
Bake at 350° for 40 minutes.

Fudgy Brownies

Nonstick cooking spray, for greasing the foil

6 oz. semisweet chocolate, chopped	1 c. all-purpose flour
	1/2 tsp. baking powder
4 oz. (1 stick) unsalted butter	1/4 tsp. salt
1 c. granulated sugar	2 oz. bittersweet chocolate,
3 large eggs	cut into pieces

Preheat the oven to 350°. Line a 9-inch square baking dish with foil and grease with cooking spray. Melt the semisweet chocolate and butter in a medium heatproof bowl set over a saucepan of simmering water, stirring occasionally until smooth. Beat together the sugar and eggs in a stand mixer on medium-high speed until creamed, about 3 minutes. Pour in the chocolate mixture and whisk until combined well. Mix in the flour, baking powder and salt for about 2 minutes on medium speed. Stir in the bittersweet chocolate chunks and transfer the batter to the prepared baking dish. Bake until the top is shiny and set and the sides have begun to pull away slightly, about 35 minutes for fudgy brownies

German Chocolate Cake- Mom

1 4 oz pkg Baker's German
brand sweet chocolate
½ c. boiling water
2 c. sugar
4 egg yolks
1 tsp. vanilla
1 c. butter or margarine

2 ¼ c. all-purpose flour,
sifted
1 tsp. soda
½ tsp. salt
1 c. buttermilk
4 egg whites, stiffly beaten

Melt chocolate in boiling water, cool. Cream butter and sugar until fluffy. Add egg yolks, 1 at a time, beating well after each. Blend in vanilla and chocolate. Sift flour with salt and soda; add alternately with buttermilk to chocolate mixture. Beat after each addition until smooth. Fold in beaten egg whites. Pour into 3 9 in pans, lined on the bottom with waxed paper. Bake at 350 for 30-35 min. Cool and frost tops and sides with Coconut Pecan Frosting.

Coconut Pecan Frosting

2 c. evaporated milk
2 c. sugar
6 egg yolks, slightly beaten
1 c. butter or margarine

2 tsp. vanilla
1 ½ C. Baker's Angel Flake
coconut
2 c. chopped pecans

Combine milk, sugar, egg yolks, butter and vanilla. Cook and stir over medium heat until thickened about 12 minutes. Add coconuts and pecans. Cool until thick enough to spread on cake, beating occasionally.

Good for You Cookies
(from friend Edith Lester)
 2 sticks real butter or margarine
2 c. brown sugar
2 eggs
2 tsp. vanilla
2 heaping serving spoons peanut butter (a serving spoon is what you'd use to serve green beans with at supper!)
2 heaping tsp. cocoa powder
1 and 1/2 c. white lily self-rising flour
1/2 c. whole wheat flour
1/4 c. millet or wheat germ
1 tsp. soda
1 tsp. baking powder
1 tsp. salt (because of the whole wheat flour, millet, and buckwheat, you still need to add baking powder and salt in these cookies even though it's already in the self-rising flour, too)
4 c. uncooked oats
1 c. chocolate chips
1 c. heath (toffee) chips
1/2 c. peanut butter chips (optional)
1/2 c. nuts--pecans or walnuts (optional)
1/2 c. unsweetened coconut (optional)

Mix in the order given above. Batter is very, very stiff once you add the oats. Stir in the chips and nuts by hand. Bake at 350°, about 10 minutes; check often in case your oven cooks faster or slower. Cookies should be taken out once they are set and before they are very brown so that they don't overcook and get hard. Makes about 4-5 dozen medium sized cookies.

Hershey's Red Velvet Sheet Cake

1/2 c. butter or margarine, softened
1 1/2 c. granulated sugar
2 large eggs
1 tsp. vanilla extract
1 c. buttermilk or sour milk *

2 T. (one 1-ounce bottle) red food color
2 c. all-purpose flour
1/3 c. HERSHEY'S Cocoa
1 tsp. salt
1 1/2 tsp. baking soda
1 T. white vinegar

Heat oven to 350°. Grease and flour 13 x 9-inch baking pan.
** Beat butter and sugar in large bowl; add eggs and vanilla, beating well.
Stir together buttermilk and food color.
Stir together flour, cocoa and salt; add alternately to butter mixture with buttermilk mixture, mixing well. Stir in baking soda and vinegar. Pour into prepared pan. Bake at 350° for 30 to 35 minutes or until wooden pick inserted in center comes out clean. Cool 10 minutes; remove from pans. Cool completely. Frost as desired.
Makes 15 servings.
* To sour milk: Use 1 tablespoon white vinegar plus milk to equal 1 cup. ** Cake can also be baked in two greased and floured 9-inch round baking pans.

Cream Cheese Frosting
1 (8 oz.) package cream cheese, softened
1 stick butter, softened

4 c. powdered sugar
1 ½ tsp. vanilla
1 T. half & half

In large bowl beat cream cheese and butter until well blended. Gradually, add powdered sugar. Stir in vanilla and half & half. Spread frosting on cooled cake. Cover and refrigerate until ready to eat.
Can be decorated with strawberries and blueberries in the shape of an American flag.

Hershey's Syrup Cake

(This recipe is from a dear, dear family friend, Gretta Lloyd. This cake has been Mom's birthday cake for many years! It never disappoints!)

1 stick butter	1 tsp. baking powder
1 c. sugar	¼ tsp. salt
4 eggs	1 (16oz.) can Hershey's
1 tsp. vanilla	chocolate syrup
1 c. flour	

Cream butter and sugar. Add eggs and vanilla. Sift flour; add baking powder and salt. Add flour mixture to the egg mixture. Add can of syrup. Bake in greased and floured 12X8X2 inch pan for 30 minutes at 350°.

Frosting:

1 stick butter	½ c. chocolate chips
1 c. sugar	1 tsp. vanilla
½ c. evaporated milk	

Melt butter. Add sugar and milk. Boil for 2 to 3 minutes. Stir in chocolate chips and vanilla. Pour over warm cake. Nuts may be added to frosting.

Homemade Milky Way Ice Cream - Lori

6 regular sized Milky Way candy bars
1 c. sugar
6 eggs
1 can Eagle brand sweetened condensed milk
1 large box of chocolate instant pudding mix
1/2 gallon whole milk

Melt candy in microwave by chopping bars in pieces, adding a little milk and putting in a microwave safe bowl. Add next four ingredients to the bowl and stir well. Pour into ice cream freezer cylinder and add milk to the "fill line" on the cylinder. Follow your ice cream maker directions for freezing.

Homemade Nutella Chocolate Ice Cream- Cathy

5 eggs
1 c. sugar
2 c. condensed milk
½ jar Nutella
Dash salt

½ pint whipping cream
3 T. vanilla extract
½ tsp. almond extract, optional

Blend first 5 ingredients together. Pour into ice cream maker cylinder and add whole milk to the "fill line" on the cylinder. Follow your ice cream maker directions for freezing. For a Cuisinart Ice Cream Maker with freezer bowl, we use the following measurements: 3 eggs, ¾ c. sugar, 1 c. condensed milk, ½ jar Nutella, dash salt, ½ pint whipping cream, 2 T. vanilla, ½ tsp. almond extract.

Homemade Peanut Butter Ice Cream- Lori

1 (16 oz.) jar crunchy peanut butter
1 c. sugar
6 eggs
1 can Eagle brand sweetened

condensed milk
1 large box vanilla instant pudding mix
1/2 gallon whole milk

Blend first 5 ingredients together. Pour into ice cream maker cylinder and add whole milk to the "fill line" on the cylinder. Follow your ice cream maker directions for freezing.

Homemade Vanilla Ice Cream- Cathy

5 eggs
1 c. sugar
2 c. condensed milk
Dash salt

½ pint whipping cream
3 T. vanilla extract
½ tsp. almond extract, optional

Blend first 5 ingredients together. Pour into ice cream maker cylinder and add whole milk to the "fill line" on the cylinder. Follow your ice cream maker directions for freezing. For a Cuisinart Ice Cream Maker with freezer bowl, we use the following measurements: 3 eggs, ¾ c. sugar, 1 c. condensed milk, dash salt, ½ pint whipping cream, 2 T. vanilla, ½ tsp. almond extract.

Italian Cream Cake- Mom

½ c. butter, softened
½ c. shortening
2 c. sugar
5 large eggs, separated
1 T. vanilla extract

2 c. all-purpose flour
1 tsp. baking soda
1 c. buttermilk
1 c. flaked coconut

Beat butter and shortening in a large mixing bowl at medium speed with an electric mixer until creamy, gradually add sugar, beating well. Add egg yolks, one at a time, beating until blended after each addition. Add vanilla, beat until blended. Combine flour and soda, add to butter mixture alternately with buttermilk, beginning and ending with flour mixture. Beat at low speed until blended after each addition. Stir in coconut. Beat egg whites until stiff peaks form, fold into batter. Pour biter into three greased and floured 9 inch round cake pans. Bake at 350° for 25 minutes or until a wooden toothpick inserted into center comes out clean. Cool in pans on wire racks 10 minutes, remove from pans, and let cool completely on wire racks.
Spread Nutty Cream Cheese Frosting between layers and on top and sides of cake.

Nutty Cream Cheese Frosting

1 c. chopped pecans
1 8-oz cream cheese, softened
½ c/ butter, softened

1 T. vanilla extract
1 16-oz package powdered sugar, sifted

Place pecans in a shallow pan, bake at 350 degrees for 5 or 10 minutes until toasted, stirring occasionally. Let cool. Beat cream cheese, butter and vanilla at medium speed until creamy. Add sugar, beating a low speed until blended. Beat at high speed until smooth, stir in pecans.

Lemonade Pie- Lori

(This is a fast and easy summertime pie)
1 can frozen lemonade concentrate, thawed (You can also substitute limeade)
1 (8 oz.) container frozen whipped topping
1 small can sweetened condensed milk
1 (9 in.) graham cracker crust
Mix together the lemonade and condensed milk. Fold in the whipped topping and pour into crust. Chill before serving. Serve with whipped topping.

No Bake Chocolate Oatmeal Cookies

1 stick butter, softened
2 c. sugar
2 T. cocoa
2/3 c. evaporated milk

½ c. peanut butter
2 c. uncooked oats
1 tsp. vanilla

Mix butter, sugar, cocoa, and mil; bring to a boil. Boil for 5 minutes. Remove from heat; add peanut butter and stir.
Add oats and vanilla, and stir quickly to coat the oats.
Drop by spoonfuls onto waxed paper. Let cool and eat.

Oatmeal Cake- Grandma Gross

Pour 1 ½ cups boiling water over 1 cup quick oats and cool. Mix 1 cup brown sugar, 1 cup white sugar and 1 stick melted butter. Add oatmeal mixture, 2 eggs and 1½ cups flour with 1 tsp. cinnamon, ½ nutmeg, 1 tsp. baking soda, and ½ tsp. salt. Add 1 tsp. vanilla. Pour in lightly greased 9 x 13 pan. Bake at 350° for 20-30 minutes.
Topping:
1 stick butter
1 c. brown sugar
1 c. chopped nuts
1 c. flaked coconut
2 eggs
Mix and add enough milk to spread. Return to oven and brown. Cool. Cut into squares.

Oatmeal Fudgies- Mom

(These have been a treat on every vacation the family has ever taken!)

1 stick butter
1 c. brown sugar (half light, half dark)
1 egg
1 tsp. vanilla
¾ c. all-purpose flour
½ tsp. soda
1/8 tsp. salt
2 c. oatmeal (quick-cooking)
½ c. chopped nuts
5 plain Hershey's bars

Cream together butter, brown sugar, egg, and vanilla. Add flour, soda, and salt; mix well. Stir in oatmeal and nuts. Spread ½ mixture into 9-inch square pan; place Hershey's bars on top. Spread rest of mix on top. Bake at 350° for 25 minutes. Cool; cut into bars.

Original Nestle Toll House Cookies

(Family favorite cookie!)

2 1/4 c. all-purpose flour
1 tsp. baking soda
1 tsp. salt
1 c. (2 sticks) butter, softened
3/4 c. granulated sugar
3/4 c. packed brown sugar
1 tsp. vanilla extract
2 large eggs
1 c. chopped nuts

2 c. (12-oz. pkg.) NESTLÉ® TOLL HOUSE® Semi-Sweet Chocolate Morsels

Preheat oven to 375°. Combine flour, baking soda and salt in small bowl. Beat butter, granulated sugar, brown sugar and vanilla extract in large mixer bowl until creamy. Add eggs, one at a time, beating well after each addition. Gradually beat in flour mixture. Stir in morsels and nuts. Drop by rounded tablespoon onto ungreased baking sheets.

Bake for 9 to 11 minutes or until golden brown. Cool on baking sheets for 2 minutes; remove to wire racks to cool completely.

SLICE AND BAKE COOKIE VARIATION:

Prepare dough as above. Divide in half; wrap in waxed paper. Refrigerate for 1 hour or until firm. Shape each half into 15-inch log; wrap in wax paper. Refrigerate for 30 minutes.* Preheat oven to 375° F. Cut into 1/2-inch-thick slices; place on ungreased

baking sheets. Bake for 8 to 10 minutes or until golden brown. Cool on baking sheets for 2 minutes; remove to wire racks to cool completely. Makes about 5 dozen cookies.
* May be stored in refrigerator for up to 1 week or in freezer for up to 8 weeks.

Peach Cobbler
Butter square or oblong casserole dish.
Pour 2 large cans peaches (drained) in dish.
Sprinkle with a mixture of ½ cup sugar, 2 T. flour, ¼ tsp cinnamon and ¼ tsp nutmeg. Dot with 2 T. butter.
Cover with pie crust. Prick crust with fork and sprinkle with sugar. Bake 30 min. at 400°.

Pecan Pie
½ c. sugar
3 T. flour (Mix with sugar.)
3 eggs, beaten

1 c. dark Karo syrup
3 T. melted butter
1 c. chopped pecans

Melt butter. Add Karo, eggs, sugar, and flour. Add nuts. Pour into unbaked pie shell. Bake 400° for 10 minutes. Then 350° for 30 minutes.

Pecan Tassies- Mom
3 oz. pkg. cream cheese, softened
½ c. butter, softened
1 c. sifted flour
Mix and let chill for 1 hour. Roll into balls – 2 doz.
Press into mini muffin tins.

1 egg
¾ c. brown sugar
1 tsp. vanilla

Dash salt
2/3 c. pecan pieces

Mix and pour into dough. Bake 325° for 20 minutes. Allow to cool a few minutes before removing.

Pumpkin Cheese Cake- Mom

3-8-oz packages cream cheese, softened
3 eggs
11/4 cups sugar
1 teaspoon cinnamon
¼ teaspoon ginger
¼ teaspoon nutmeg
1 teaspoon grated lemon rind (optional)
1 can (15-16 oz.) pumpkin

Beat at medium speed the cream cheese in an electric mixer. Add other ingredients slowly in order. When ingredients are completely mixed place in 9" baking dish over the crust prepared earlier. Bake at 300° for 1 ¼ hours.

Crust
2 cups graham crackers rolled and finely crushed.
¼ cup sugar
1/3 cup margarine (melted)
11/2 teaspoon cinnamon
½ teaspoon nutmeg

Mix all ingredients together until mixture can hold its shape. Line bottom and edge of baking dish and place pumpkin mix over it.

Pumpkin Crunch Cake

1 (15 oz.) can pumpkin puree
1 (12 fluid oz.) can evaporated milk
4 eggs
1 ½ c. white sugar
2 tsp. pumpkin pie spice
1 tsp. salt
1 (18.25 oz.) package yellow cake mix
1 c. chopped pecans
1 c. butter, melted

Preheat oven to 350°. Lightly grease one 9x13 inch baking pan. In a large bowl, combine pumpkin, evaporated milk, eggs, sugar, pumpkin pie spice, and salt. Mix well, and spread into the prepared pan. Sprinkle cake mix over the top of the pumpkin mixture, and pat down. Sprinkle chopped pecans evenly over the cake mix, then drizzle with melted butter.
Bake for 60 to 80 minutes, or until done. Top with whipping cream when ready to serve.

Pumpkin Pie

¾ c. sugar
½ tsp. salt
1 tsp. ground cinnamon
½ tsp ground ginger

¼ tsp. ground cloves
2 large eggs
1 can (15 oz.) 100% pure
pumpkin

1 c. (12 oz.) evaporated milk
1 unbaked 9-inch deep-dish
pie shell

Mix sugar, salt, cinnamon, ginger, and cloves in small bowl. Beat eggs in large bowl. Stir in pumpkin and sugar-spice mixture. Gradually stir in evaporated milk. Pour into pie shell. Bake in preheated 425° oven for 15 minutes. Reduce temperature to 350°; bake 40-50 minutes or until knife inserted near center comes out clean. Cool on wire rack for 2 hours. Serve immediately or refrigerate.

Rice Pudding

1 ¼ c. cooked rice
2 eggs
2 c. milk
1 c. raisins
¼ c. sugar

¼ tsp. salt
1 tsp. vanilla
Dash cinnamon
Dash nutmeg

Beat eggs till light and thick. Fold in milk; mix rest of ingredients. Place in buttered 1 ½ qt. casserole 350° for 1 hour in shallow pan of water.

Simple Cheesecake

Grease 8x8 pan.
Crust:
1 ½ c. crushed graham
cracker
6 T. melted butter

½ c. medium finely chopped
nuts
¼ c. sugar

Mix and press into the bottom of the 8x8 pan. Bake 350° for 6 – 8 minutes. Cool.
Filling:
2 (8 oz.) pkgs. cream cheese
1 c. sugar
2 large eggs, beaten

8 oz. sour cream
1 tsp. vanilla

Mix and pour into cooled crust. Bake 350° for 35 minutes. Let stand in oven 1 hour. Refrigerate.

S'More Bars

1/2 c. unsalted butter, room temperature
1/4 c. brown sugar
1/2 c. granulated sugar
1 large egg, room temperature
1 tsp. vanilla extract
1 1/3 c. all-purpose flour

3/4 c. graham cracker crumbs (about 8 graham crackers)
1 tsp. baking powder
1/4 tsp. salt
2 king-sized milk chocolate bars

1 1/2 c. marshmallow Fluff (not melted marshmallows because they harden when they cool).

Preheat oven to 350 degrees F. Grease and/or line an 8-inch square baking pan. In a large bowl, cream together butter and sugar until light. Beat in egg and vanilla. In a small bowl, whisk together flour, graham cracker crumbs, baking powder and salt. Add to butter mixture and mix at a low speed until combined. Divide dough in half and press half of dough into an even layer on the bottom of the prepared pan. Don't worry if it seems thin; the baking powder will allow it to rise. Place chocolate bars over dough (don't layer the bars, just break them to fit if you need to), then spread the marshmallow Fluff over the chocolate bars. Finally, top the Fluff with the remaining dough by forming the dough into sheets with the palm of your hands and laying it down (as shown above). Don't worry if the dough isn't covering everything! It'll spread out as it bakes. Bake for 30 to 35 minutes, until lightly browned. If the top is browning too quickly, you can always cover it with tin foil for the remaining baking time. Cool completely before cutting into bars. If you don't allow them to cool completely, they will crumble when you try to cut them. Makes 16-20 bars.

Sock-It-To-Me Cake

(This was Chuck's favorite coffee cake. Mom made it for him to take on his family vacations.)

1 box Duncan Hines Butter Recipe Golden Cake Mix
1 c. sour cream
1/3 c. canola oil
¼ c. sugar

¼ c. water
4 eggs

Filling:
1 c. chopped pecans
2 T. brown sugar

2 tsp. cinnamon

Preheat oven to 375°. In a large mixing bowl blend together the cake mix, sour cream, oil, ¼ c. sugar, water, and eggs. Beat at high speed for 2 minutes. Pour 2/3 of all the batter in a greased and buttered 10" tube pan. Combine filling ingredients and sprinkle over batter in pan. Spoon the remaining batter evenly over pecans. Bake 40 minutes or until toothpick inserted in center comes out clean. Cool cake on wire rack 25 minutes. Remove cake from pan and cool completely.

Sour Cream Lemon Pie

1 c. sugar
3 T. cornstarch
¼ c. butter
1 T. grated lemon rind
1 cooked refrigerator pie crust

¼ c. lemon juice
3 egg yolks, unbeaten
1 c. milk
1 c. sour cream

In saucepan, combine sugar, cornstarch, butter, lemon rind, lemon juice and egg yolks; mix well. Blend in milk and cook over medium heat, stirring constantly, until thick. Cool; add to sour cream a little at a time, stirring until smooth. Spoon into cooled shell and chill at least 2 hours before serving.

Southern Living Banana Pudding Pie

1 (12oz) box vanilla wafers, divided
½ c. melted butter
Vanilla Cream filling
4 egg whites

2 large bananas, sliced

½ c. sugar

Set aside 30 vanilla wafers; pulse remaining vanilla wafers in a food processor 8-10 minutes until crushed. You should have 2 ½ cups after crushing. Stir together crushed wafers and butter until blended. Firmly press on bottom, up sides of the 9" pie plate. Bake at 350° for 10-12 minutes until lightly browned. Let cool 30 minutes. Arrange banana slices evenly over bottom of crust. Prepare vanilla cream filling.

Vanilla Cream Filling
¾ c. sugar
1/3 c. all-purpose flour
2 large eggs

4 egg yolks
2 c. milk
2 tsp. vanilla extract

Whisk first 5 ingredients together in saucepan. Cook over medium heat, whisking constantly 8-10 minutes or until it reaches the consistence of pudding. Remove from heat and stir in vanilla. Spread half of the filling over bananas; top with 20 vanilla wafers. Beat egg whites on high until they are foamy. Add sugar, 1 Tbsp. at a time, beating until stiff peaks form and sugar dissolves. Spread meringue evenly over hot filling, sealing the edges. Bake at 350° for 10-12 minutes until brown. Let cool for an hour. Coarsely crush remaining 10 vanilla wafers and sprinkle evenly over top of pie. Chill 4 hours before serving.

Strawberry Cake- Mom

1 pkg. white cake mix
1 (3 oz.) pkg. strawberry Jell-O
½ (10 oz.) pkg. frozen strawberries

1 c. Canola oil
½ c. water
4 eggs

Mix cake mix and Jell-O. Beat in eggs. Add other ingredients. Bake in 2 layer cake pans. Bake about 30 minutes at 350°; test for doneness.

Icing:
1 stick butter
1 box confectioners' sugar
Mix and spread on cool cake.

½ (10 oz.) pkg. frozen strawberries

Strawberry Pie - Lori

9" pie shell (I use Pillsbury refrigerated)
4 c. strawberries washed, hulled, and sliced in half
1½ c. water
¾ c. sugar
2 Tbsp. cornstarch
1 (3 oz.) pkg. strawberry Jell-O

Bake pie shell according to package directions. Cool. Place washed and hulled strawberries in cool pie shell. Combine water, sugar and cornstarch in a saucepan. Bring to boil and cook two minutes. Add strawberry Jell-O and stir until dissolved. Pour over berries. Chill until set. Serve with homemade whipped cream

Strawberry Shortcake Cake

9 T. unsalted butter, softened, plus more for greasing
1 1/2 c. flour, plus more for dusting
3 T. cornstarch
1 tsp. baking soda
1/2 tsp. salt
1 1/2 c. plus two tablespoons sugar
3 whole large eggs
1/2 c. sour cream, at room temperature
1 tsp. vanilla extract
1 lb. strawberries, plus more to garnish
Icing
1 1/2 lbs. powdered sugar, sifted
8 oz. cream cheese, at room temperature
2 sticks unsalted butter
1 tsp. vanilla extract
Salt

Special equipment: 8-inch cake pan that's at least 2-inches deep. Preheat the oven to 350°. Grease and flour an 8-inch cake pan. Sift together flour, cornstarch, baking soda and salt. In stand mixer fitted with a paddle attachment, cream the butter with 1 1/2 cups of the sugar until light and fluffy. Add the eggs one at a time, mixing well after each addition. Add the sour cream and vanilla, and mix until combined. Add the sifted dry ingredients and mix on low speed until just barely combined. Pour the batter into the prepared cake pan. Bake until no longer jiggly like my bottom, 45 to 50 minutes. Remove the cake from the pan as soon as you pull it out of the oven. Place the cake on a cooling rack and allow it to cool completely. Stem the strawberries and mash them. Sprinkle the strawberries with the remaining 2 tablespoons sugar and allow to sit for 30 minutes.

For the icing: Combine the powdered sugar, cream cheese, butter, vanilla and dash of salt in a mixing bowl. Mix until very light and fluffy.

Slice the cake in half to make two smaller cakes. Spread the strawberries evenly over each cut side of cake, pouring on all the juices as well. Place the cake halves into the freezer for 5 minutes, just to make icing the cake easier.

Remove the cake halves from the freezer. Use a little less than one-third of the icing to spread over the top of the strawberries on the bottom layer. Place the second layer of cake on top. Add half of the remaining icing to the top spreading evenly, then spread the remaining icing around the sides. Leave plain or garnish with strawberry halves, serve slightly cool. This cake is best when served slightly cool. The butter content in the icing will cause it to soften at room temperature. For best results, store in the fridge!

Sugar Cookies - Mom

Slightly less than 1 ½ c. all-purpose flour
½ tsp. baking soda
¼ tsp. baking powder

½ c. butter, softened
¾ c. sugar
1 egg
½ tsp. vanilla extract

Preheat oven to 375°. In a small bowl, stir together flour, baking soda, and baking powder. Set aside. In a large bowl, cream together the butter and sugar until smooth. Beat in egg and vanilla. Gradually blend in the dry ingredients. Roll rounded teaspoons full of dough into balls and place onto ungreased cookie sheets. OR roll the dough into a sheet and use cookie cutters to cut out cookies. Bake 8 to 10 minutes or until golden.

Texas Sheet Cake

3 T. cocoa
2 sticks (1 c.) butter or margarine

1 c. water

Combine this in a saucepan. Bring to boil, then remove from heat. Set aside.

½ c. buttermilk
2 eggs
1 tsp. baking soda
Pinch of salt

1 tsp. vanilla extract
2 c. sugar
2 c. plain all-purpose flour

Mix these ingredients together, then add to above mixture. Mix well. Pour into an ungreased jellyroll pan (mine is 12" x 17"). Bake for 15 minutes in an oven preheated to 400°.
While cake is baking, make icing.

Icing:
1 stick (1/2 c.) butter or margarine
2 T. cocoa
6 T. buttermilk

1 tsp. vanilla extract
1 box powdered sugar (10x)
1 c. chopped pecans (optional)

Melt butter and cocoa in a medium saucepan. Add remaining ingredients. Mix well. Keep icing warm until cake is done baking. Ice cake while it is hot.

Tiramisu

6 egg yolks
1/2 c. white sugar
2 tsp. vanilla extract
2 c. mascarpone cheese

24 ladyfingers
2 c. brewed coffee
1 T. cocoa powder

In a medium bowl, beat yolks with sugar and vanilla until smooth and light yellow and very fluffy. Fold mascarpone into yolk mixture. Set aside. Dip ladyfingers briefly in coffee and arrange 12 of them in the bottom of a 10×10 inch dish. Spread half the mascarpone mixture over the ladyfingers. Repeat with remaining cookies and mascarpone.
Cover and chill 1 hour. Sprinkle with cocoa just before serving.

Viennese Crescent Cookies - Mom

2 sticks butter, softened
¾ c. sugar
1 ½ tsp. vanilla
Stir well. Add 2 ½ c. sifted flour and 1 c. nuts. Work well with fingers. Make large ball. Form small balls and place on lightly greased cookie sheet. Bake 350° for 15 minutes. Cool 1 minute. Roll in powdered sugar twice.

Yellow Cake with Chocolate Icing

1 c. butter	1 ½ tsp. vanilla extract
1 ½ c. sugar	2 c. flour
8 egg yolks	2 tsp. baking powder
¾ c. milk	½ tsp. salt

Preheat oven to 350°. Grease and flour 2 8" round pans. Sift together the flour, baking powder and salt. Set aside. In a large bowl, cream together the butter and sugar until light and fluffy. Beat in the egg yolks one at a time; then stir in the vanilla. Beat in the flour mixture alternately with the milk, mixing just until incorporated. Pour batter into prepared pans. Bake in the preheated oven for 25-30 minutes, or until tops spring back when lightly tapped. Cool 15 minutes before turning out onto cooling racks.

Chocolate Icing

4 T. butter	1 T. unsweetened cocoa
½ c. packed brown sugar	powder
2 T. milk	1 tsp. vanilla extract
1 ½ c. confectioner's sugar	

In a saucepan melt butter and brown sugar over medium heat. Stir until sugar is dissolved, then add milk. Bring to a boil and remove from heat. Sift together cocoa and confectioner's sugar. Blend into butter mixture and add vanilla. If consistency is too stiff, add more milk. Spread quickly over cooled cake, as frosting will set up very fast.

Balsamic Vinaigrette - Cathy

1 c. canola oil
½ c. balsamic vinegar
½ c. sugar

Dash of garlic powder
Couple dashes Heinz 57
steak sauce

(To make Red Wine Vinaigrette, substitute red wine vinegar for balsamic vinegar.)

Bleu Cheese Dressing

2 c. mayonnaise
½ T. grated onion
½ tsp. white pepper
½ tsp. garlic powder
1 tsp. lemon juice
1 tsp. Worcestershire sauce

1/8 c. buttermilk
1/8 c. white vinegar
4 oz. crumbled bleu cheese
1 tsp. parsley flakes
1 tsp. salt
1 tsp. sugar

Combine all ingredients and stir well.

Blueberry Pancakes

1 c. all-purpose flour
½ c. graham cracker crumbs
1 T. sugar
1 tsp. baking powder
½ tsp. baking soda
¼ tsp. salt

2 eggs, lightly beaten
1 ¼ c. buttermilk
¼ c. butter, melted
1 c. fresh or frozen
blueberries

Topping:
 1 (3 oz.) pkg. cream cheese, softened
¾ c. whipped cream

For topping, in a small bowl, beat cream cheese and whipped cream until smooth. Chill until serving. In a large bowl, combine the flour, cracker crumbs, sugar, baking powder, baking soda, and salt. Combine the eggs, buttermilk and butter; add to dry ingredients just until moistened. Fold in blueberries. Pour batter by ¼ cupfuls onto a greased hot griddle (approx. 350°). Turn when bubbles form on top. Cook until the4 second side is golden brown. Spread topping over pancakes. Top with warm syrup; sprinkle with additional blueberries if desired.

Buttery Sauce for Grilled Chicken
1 stick butter
½ tsp. garlic powder
1 T. cider vinegar
1 T. celery seed
1 T. dry mustard

Citrus Balsamic Glaze for Salmon
3 T. balsamic vinegar   1 T. orange juice
1 ½ T. cornstarch   1 T. brown sugar
Mix in saucepan until thick and spread over salmon.

Honey Mustard Dressing - Chuck
1 c. mayo
¾ c. sour cream
¼ c. honey
3-4 T Dijon mustard (to taste)
Blend and chill.

Nuts 'n Bolts
8 T. butter, melted   3/8 tsp. garlic powder
4 tsp. Worchester sauce
Combine in 9x13 inch pan. Add the following:
6 c. mixture of rice, wheat, and corn Chex cereal
1 c. Cheerios   1 can mixed nuts
Bake at 250° for 45 minutes. Stir every 15 minutes. Spread on paper towels until cool.

Peanut Clusters
1 package (6 ounces) semi-sweet chocolate chips
1 package (6 ounces) peanut butter chips
1 small can (6 ½ ounces) cocktail peanuts
Melt chips in casserole dish on medium-high 3-4 minutes. Stir until smooth. Add nuts. Stir until well-coated. Drop by teaspoonful onto waxed paper. Cool until firm. Yield: 4 dozen

Pimento Cheese

Shred 1 block sharp cheddar cheese. Mix in the following:

¾ c. mayonnaise (I use
Duke's.)
Large jar of pimentos
(drained)

Dash of
Worcestershire sauce
Dash of salt

Poppy Seed Dressing

1 ½ c. sugar
2 tsp. dry mustard
2/3 c. vinegar

1 T. grated white onion
2 c. canola oil
3 T. poppy seeds

Mix and store overnight. Shake well before serving. Keeps for several months.

Sausage Gravy

1 package sausage*
¼ c. flour

2 ½ c. milk
Salt and pepper to taste

*(We are partial to fresh Sand Mountain, Alabama, sausage near our home but choose your favorite.)

Cook sausage in large skillet over medium heat 5-6 minutes or until thoroughly heated, stirring frequently. Stir in flour. Gradually add milk; cook until mixture comes to a boil and thickens, stirring constantly. Reduce heat to medium-low; simmer 2 minutes, stirring constantly. Season to taste with salt and pepper.

Turkey Gravy

Heat 4 c. turkey broth.

¾ c. flour in 1 ½ c. water: mix and pour through small strainer into the broth before broth gets too hot.

Add the following:

1 c. milk
½ c. evaporated milk

1 T. butter
Salt and pepper to taste

Stir constantly until it begins to boil. If it is too thick, add more milk. If it is too thin, add more flour paste.

Whipping Cream (You better not put a frozen whipped topping on our desserts!)

1 c. heavy cream   1 T. confectioners' sugar
1 tsp. vanilla extract

In a large bowl, whip cream until stiff peaks are just about to form. Beat in vanilla and sugar until peaks form. Make sure not to over-beat, or cream will become lumpy and butter-like.

Tidbits

Here are some tidbits we need to tell ya'll. If it's absolutely necessary (besides New Year's Day) to use paper products, spend the extra dollar and get some with some durability. OK?

Paper plates – Chinette oval (Chinette because nobody wants their food to soak through their plate and oval because, yes, it needs to be a big one.)

Napkins – heavy duty DINNER napkins (Nobody wants cheap paper napkin shards all over their face.)

Cups – Solo brand (Nobody wants to be the one who dropped their cup because it was so cheap they couldn't hang on to it)

Utensils – THERE IS NEVER AN OCASSION TO USE PLASTIC UTENSILS. (If you inferred those capital letters to be hollerin', you were correct.)

Last, certainly not least, the key to any good gathering is conversation! Always relive the good ole days – those are the best tales! The younger ones need to hear their heritage and every time you're together is fodder for the future generation.

Eat, drink sweet tea, and be merry!

Index

BREADS & ROLLS   p. 135

About the Authors

Dr. Cathy Robbs Baker serves as Director of Education at Christ United Methodist Church in Chattanooga, Tennessee, where she fulfills her passion of supporting people in their journey of faith. She finds great fulfillment in leading Bible study groups Women of Worth and Mom2Mom and helping women find God's purpose in their lives. She was named a 2016 Chattanooga Woman of Distinction. Prior to her church work, Dr. Turner was a high school English teacher and Change Coach. Holding a doctorate in Education: Learning and Leadership, she also serves as an organizational and faith development coach, and organizes national and international group travel. In her book *Looking Forward* she shares her faith journey as she coped with cancer, divorce, and then the death of a spouse. Visit her inspirational blog at www.leadingforward.us to read her weekly devotions. She is the proud "mother" of two handsome sons, two beautiful daughters-in-law, and the stars of the family, grandchildren Stella and Will. She enjoys reading, writing, traveling, and singing. Her ideal day is spent riding through the mountains enjoying God's scenery!

Lori Gross Kelley is a native of Chattanooga, TN and southern to the core. She has been married to her husband, Mark, for 32 years and has two children, Chase and Kaitlin, whom she counts as her two greatest accomplishments. Over the past 30 years, she has worked in the medical field in several different capacities, most recently in the area of administration. This is where she finds her best opportunities to share her faith – with those who could use some spiritual healing, uplifting, a listening ear, or just a dose of good humor. As an adult, with her children in college, Lori enrolled in the University of Tennessee at Chattanooga to pursue a degree in English. She earned a Bachelor of Arts in English, American Language and Literature and a minor in Business Administration. As a platform to encourage others, she uses her four year journey of being an adult student balancing family, education, and career to encourage others to claim Philippians 4:13 and aspire to inspire. She is active in local music and theatre productions and a frequent traveler to the beach.

Made in the USA
Monee, IL
29 December 2023